TOGETHER **STRONG**

A mother and daughter share a canceled wedding,
a charity event, and all that followed

Patty Carbee and Kyle Paxman

authorHOUSE®

AuthorHouse™
1663 Liberty Drive
Bloomington, IN 47403
www.authorhouse.com
Phone: 1-800-839-8640

First published by AuthorHouse   7/11/2011

ISBN: 978-1-4634-1317-0 (hc)
ISBN: 978-1-4634-1318-7 (e)
ISBN: 978-1-4634-1319-4 (sc)

Library of Congress Control Number: 2011909756

Printed in the United States of America

Together Strong is dedicated to Sherwood Charles Carbee.

You were an amazing husband and father who taught us how to live life to its fullest. Until the end you were brave, strong, and proud.

We love you – the world and some!

Patty and Kyle

Chapter I

The water is still, the sun is shining bright and I'm feeling so relaxed! Each time I look out over the expanse of Lake Champlain I think of my father's assessment of Vermont: God's Country, the most beautiful place on earth. As I sit here and reflect, I understand exactly what he meant!

Sometimes on this journey of life I wonder why things happen the way they do. But regardless of all that has and all that might yet happen, I always try to keep a positive attitude. If life is what we make it, I'm going to work towards the happy ending!

Over the years, raising my two children, this is a belief I've tried to pass on to them. Fortunately, they embraced this concept of keeping a positive attitude, and as you'll soon discover it has helped us through some very hard times…

PATTY

The title of my job may sound boring to you. I'm the Senior Vice President of Marketing and Business Development for a major life insurance company. To me however it has been an exciting career filled with great opportunities. I've mostly been very happy with the work I do, and always proud of the results.

I may have questioned this over the last few weeks as I spent nights and weekends working in an effort to prepare my boss for an executive planning meeting that will take place during my vacation – time I also spent keeping other projects moving along and on schedule. It has frankly been exhausting and I can't wait to take off for vacation.

Some background: My boss is fairly new to the company. He has been with us less than a year and I have to admit I've been struggling to work well with him. In fact, I have never experienced working with anyone quiet like him during my 30-plus years in the industry.

I have gained a reputation as one of the best marketing minds in the business, yet he doesn't seem to see the value in anything I do. He is having me spend my days defining and mapping processes. Ugh! Clearly this is important to the company, but it is not helping to generate sales, which is the life blood of our industry.

Our team, Sales and Marketing, is in the process of redefining its strategy. Something we seem to do every few years. My boss is scheduled to present our conclusions at the executive planning meeting. He is also responsible for presenting our completed processes, including our "gap analysis" and recommendations. I know he isn't prepared – and as a perfectionist this freaks me out – especially since he is representing the entire marketing team. I'm looking at this as my opportunity to demonstrate my value and help him look good in front of the executive team. Which is why I was happy to work like a crazy woman over the past few weeks – I was delivering for him what no one else could. He would be well-positioned for the executive team meeting, and I could leave on vacation feeling good about my contribution.

My husband Sherwood left a few days earlier with our dog, Ernie. He will get the lake cottage ready, do the grocery shopping, and of course, stock the bar. When I arrive it will be time to just sit back and relax for the next two weeks. I can hardly wait!

We love the lake cottage. It is in Alburgh, Vermont about as far north as you can get, just minutes from the New York state line and the Canadian border. Having lived in Vermont for most of our lives, being there is also a chance to spend time with family and friends.

This year vacation is going to be a little different as we are also in the middle of planning our daughter's wedding. Kyle lives in Cardiff-by-the-Sea, California and her wedding will be at the Basin Harbor Club in Vergennes, Vermont in just six weeks! What an exciting time. I have loved every minute of planning her event. I am her wedding coordinator and it is going to be a wedding to remember – the wedding of her dreams. Truly—her job is to dream it and my job is to make it happen. And I have to say it has been great for me to have something fun and exciting to work on away from the office. It has helped ease my frustrations and enjoy my creativity.

A little about my daughter – the bride to be, Kyle turned 29 in May. What a beautiful woman she is. At five feet, four inches her petite figure, blond hair and amazing smile makes her stand out in a crowd. She got engaged nine months ago to Kurt, whom she has been dating for almost four years now. What a catch! He is tall dark and handsome, with a great job – and boy does he love Kyle. As a parent, I couldn't ask for more than that. We are ecstatic that he will soon be our son-in-law.

My son Keith will turn 32 in two weeks. He got married four years ago to Julia and they now have a beautiful daughter named McKenna Marie. Sherwood's two children, Doug and Sherri, are also happily married. Kyle will be our last to walk down the aisle. We are looking forward to having all of the kids settled down. Somehow, you seem to worry a little less about them when they have a family of their own. I'm not sure why, but it's true for me at least.

As I lock up the house and head out for Vermont I get the same feeling of excitement that only comes over me when I know I'm heading home!

The time will fly by as I spend the seven hour ride from Pennsylvania to Vermont planning my week – I love a plan! I only have two weeks of vacation and so much to do. Besides scheduling time with family, I need to contact the Vermont Symphony Orchestra to confirm the music they will play during the wedding. I will call Basin Harbor Club with our final count and seating chart, and then review the ceremony with Keith and the Justice of the Peace. That's a funny story in itself.

Kyle scheduled the Justice of the Peace, a wonderful older gentlemen with a good track record (he assured us)! But since we'd selected him at random and he didn't really know who Kyle was, we had asked Keith to be a part of the ceremony. Keith we lovingly refer to now as Reverend Keith – went online, completed the paperwork and became ordained. It was a very simple process that took only a few minutes and cost just $25. Unfortunately, as we later learned, the State of Vermont doesn't recognize online credentials. So we still needed our Justice of the Peace. Keith, however, would do the majority of the speaking. (I wonder if Joey from the TV series Friends knows that many states are not recognizing these ceremonies as legally binding.) Well, regardless, we were going to do it right.

As if planning a wedding and squeezing in time with Sherwood isn't enough to fill two weeks, I am also scheduled to attend a bridal shower for my niece, Misty, who will be getting married in October. The day after that I am flying out to see Kyle to attend her California bridal shower, planned by her maid of honor, Lisa. The gifts are going to be "honeymoon" packages. Kyle and Kurt have planned a wonderful Tahitian honeymoon.

I will then return to Vermont to enjoy my last few days on the lake before heading back to the reality of the office.

I was excited to get going! I was about one hour into my ride when I started thinking about last year's vacation, at this very time and place, when I'd received a call from my former boss (whom I loved) telling me that he had just resigned. In our business and at his level, "resigned" is simply the nice way of saying you've just been replaced. I remember being so sad to hear he was going to be leaving. We had always worked great together – life wouldn't be the same without him. Boy, were those thoughts on target! I've been sorry every day since he left. What were they thinking when they hired the man that replaced him?

Perhaps when I'm more relaxed I can think of the relationship I have with Peter and see if I can't find a way to make working with him more productive, if not enjoyable. But I refuse to follow the lead of some of the others on the team. I'm not a butt kisser. It has always been my belief that hard work and delivering results should be enough to gain trust and respect. But that doesn't seem to be the case with this guy.

Deep into my own thoughts and making pretty good time on the road, my cell phone begins to ring.

KYLE

I can't believe my wedding is just weeks away. What an exciting time! Kurt and I are so happy and everything is coming together perfectly.

The invitations went out several weeks ago and the responses are starting to come in. We are thrilled that so many of our friends and family are going to be with us. Friends from all over the country – California, Washington, Maryland, Georgia, South Carolina, Pennsylvania, New York, New Hampshire, Vermont and St. John in the U.S. Virgin Islands. When we made the decision to have our wedding in Vermont it really became a destination wedding for many. So, we had a block of rooms reserved at The Basin Harbor Club to accommodate those who wanted to make it a long weekend – or even a week of vacation.

We originally blocked 25 rooms, but now we are up to 45 and counting. There is little to do now but wait for the day to arrive.

I will go to Vermont the week of the wedding and join my parents at the lake house for a few days, and then Mom and I will head over to the Basin Harbor Club to finalize all the details.

Kurt is scheduled to arrive on Wednesday. He is going to spend the night at the cottage with Dad. I've been amazed at how well Kurt and Dad get along. Growing up, Dad was never a fan of my boyfriends. But these two get along great and they are looking forward to spending a guy's night together - steaks on the grill and drinks down at the dock. We have assigned them only one job: they have to pick up all of the tuxedos on Thursday morning before they join us.

Most guests will arrive on Thursday, September 7th, so the morning of the 8th our planned activities will begin. My brother Keith is hosting a golf tournament for the guys. My sister-in-law Julia will host a beach party for the girls. The rehearsal party is planned for the evening. We will walk through the ceremony at the wedding arch, and then everyone in the wedding party and our immediate family members are going on a cocktail cruise. Two of Kurt's friends are musicians and will entertain us while onboard. When we dock, Kurt's brother-in-law will lead us off the cruise boat in his Scottish garb playing the bag-pipes. The rest of our guests will be there waiting. My future in-laws have planned an amazing barbeque which, if all goes well, will include a great sun set!

Saturday morning I can only imagine how I'll be feeling – it will be the big day. The one I have dreamed of since I was a little girl. I want to enjoy and embrace every minute of the day. It may be a little superstitious – but once I leave the rehearsal dinner I don't want to see Kurt again until I'm walking down the aisle!

Mom and I scheduled the beauticians to come to the resort to do our hair. I have my something old and borrowed all picked out (a diamond hairpin my father bought for my mother at an antique shop years ago); something new (my beautiful Carolina Herrera custom designed gown); and something blue (a topaz and diamond necklace my mother bought for me during a trip the two of us had taken to San Francisco earlier this year.) I was ready!

The perfect wedding has been planned – I know that even the Vermont weather will cooperate with me. The wedding ceremony and the cocktail reception will both be held outside. The setting is going to be amazing! Our guests will be handed beautifully designed programs and they'll sip on lemonade and apple cider as they listen to a trio from the Vermont Symphony Orchestra. I will walk down the marble path from what soon will be the honeymoon suite to the wedding arch. With a father on each side – my biological father Mike on my left and the Dad who raised me – Sherwood – on my right. When we get half way down the aisle I'll say good-by to Mike and Dad will walk me the rest of the way and give me away.

Our guest will have an amazing view looking west across Lake Champlain to the Adirondack Mountains. This is going to be quite the back drop for the formal wedding pictures, which will be taken immediately following the ceremony as our guests are escorted to a cocktail reception where they'll enjoy hot and cold hors d'orderves, an open bar, and background music by the same trio.

I'm pretty sure we have thought of everything – the satin trunk for wedding cards will be the centerpiece of the gift table. The place cards are silver frames with the date *September 9, 2006* engraved on the bottom. Beautiful flowers and tea lights will decorate each table. We even have battery powered lights to place under each table to add an illumination that will make the room sparkle for our guests. We have a printed menu at each place setting and the wedding cake will be simple but elegant with fresh flowers matching my bouquet.

Other than the ceremony itself, the part Kurt and I are most excited about is the band. We both love reggae and we have booked a five piece group from Maryland to perform. We heard their tape and they are amazing. It was a lot of fun putting our list of songs together – the ones we want to make sure are played.

We also decided that we don't want to follow many of the usual wedding traditions. There will be no special dance. No tossing of the bouquet or garter (in fact there won't be a garter) and we will quietly cut the wedding cake – no cake feeding for us!

So many plans, well thought out plans, are now in place. Every day I wake up thinking of the wedding and either call or email Mom to see what's going on. I feel so lucky that she has the skills and the desire to handle all of this for me. She has actually told me that she's thankful to have had something she's so excited about doing – evidently work hasn't been much fun for her lately. Yes – I'm certain that everything will be perfect!!!

Following the wedding we are going to Tahiti for ten days. My maid-of-honor is a travel agent and she has helped us put our plan in place. We will fly back to San Diego on Monday morning and fly out of LA for Tahiti on Tuesday. One night in Tahiti, three nights in Moorea and six nights in Bora Bora – fun in the sun will be the perfect ending!

There have only been two bumps in the road so far. When the dresses we had ordered for my bridal party arrived they didn't look as good on the girls as they had on-line. We then had to scurry around to find a replacement that everyone would like. Fortunately we did and they had just arrived. Our second bump came when the responses started coming in. Three of Kurt's very best friends responded that they couldn't attend. Kurt was crushed to think that they had decided to attend a college football game instead of attending our wedding. Then his best girlfriend responded that she couldn't make it either – she had a work conflict. I felt so bad for Kurt, but I did my best to make him feel better about it. In the end he shared with Mom that as long as he was marrying the love of his life it really wasn't important who was there to see it. He's so sweet!

He was down in the dumps for a little while but he perked right up when we picked up our wedding rings. They were amazing! We had them designed by the same jeweler that made my engagement ring. We were both so excited when we picked them up that we called our mothers and then had a celebration drink. September 9th would be here before we knew it!

One more thing: Kurt and I have a secret that we can't wait to share with our parents. No – I'm not pregnant. Although that is something I do look forward to within the next couple of years. But we are still very excited about our news. Both of our families are back East and soon after we return from our honeymoon we are going home! Kurt's company is giving him a transfer that will put us in Cape May, New Jersey. He's already told his parents but I am going to surprise mine the week of the wedding. Since graduating from college I've always lived far away – first to St. John in the Virgin Islands, then to Charleston, South Carolina, and now on the West Coast. I know they will be thrilled to have us closer.

Our lives really are coming together – for better or for worse, in sickness and in health, until death do us part. Words I can hardly wait to exchange!

∾ Chapter II ∾

KYLE

Today is Friday, July 28th and my mother is leaving Pennsylvania for vacation in Vermont – Dad and Ernie have been there for a few days already. Knowing Dad he has everything ready so that Mom can just walk in and relax for the next two weeks. I wish I could be there with them. I love the cottage and being on the lake is so comforting.

As I think of it now, it occurs to me that last year I unexpectedly joined them on their vacation. I know that at this time every year I'll be reminded of a tragedy that took place just one year earlier. A beautiful young woman that worked for me died suddenly and unexpectedly. In her early 20's she had so much life to live, but enjoying the water's edge one evening she slipped and fell to her death. I was devastated. She was a great person – I couldn't imagine the pain her family had to be feeling. I took care of everything that had to be done at work and spent some time with her family. It was so sad, but her passing helped me realize the importance of family – and I knew at the time that I really wanted to be with mine. When I called to talk Mom didn't hesitate. She told me to get a ticket and come to Vermont. And that's just what I did. I caught the next flight out.

Reuniting with my family and being on the lake during that stressful time was just what I needed. I was in the best possible place. I was able to pay tribute to the memory of my friend and celebrate the love of my family. The lake has always had a healing effect on me.

I know that Mom and Dad will have a great vacation this year. Mom has been feeling worn out from work and I know she is looking forward to getting away. She is also pretty excited about finalizing the wedding arrangements. I think planning my wedding has been a dream of hers as well as mine. She never had a big wedding herself.

I made a note to remind myself to call them later but for now, I have to get to work. I have a management meeting this morning!

When I arrived at work I went right to my meeting. As I was sitting around the table with the rest of the team we received a phone call. I was so surprised when my boss said it was for me, and that I had friends outside who were waiting to see me. This was odd – I couldn't imagine that any of my friends would have me pulled out of a management meeting. So, I gave my report and then was excused.

I went to the Spa Café but I didn't see anyone I knew. So, I just began the regular routine. I gave the usual instructions to the staff and began arranging the tables so they could be set for the day. As I was working, a young man and woman approached me.

The man was tall, dark and handsome. The woman was also very attractive. Clearly I would remember them if we had met before. The man introduced himself as Jon, and asked if I was Kyle. I shook his hand and asked if we had met before. He confirmed that we had not. His next question surprised and scared me. He asked, "Are you engaged to Kurt who works for Milestone?" As I acknowledged that I was, a feeling of panic started to set in. "Is he ok, did something awful happen to him?" Jon was quick to assure me that Kurt was alright, but he needed to share something with me. So, I asked them to have a seat.

Jon began his story. He was sorry to have to tell me this, but my fiancée had been having an affair for the past six weeks with his former girlfriend. As he continued to speak, my mind kept telling me, "no, this cannot be real, he must be mistaken. I'm getting married in just a few more weeks." But quickly remembering where we were and who might be within earshot, I asked Jon if we could talk somewhere else. I did not want to have this conversation in front of my staff. So we walked to the parking lot and sat in his truck where he continued to share the details with me.

He had been dating "Sharron" for nearly five years, and was contemplating getting engaged himself. But he had a few suspicions, a kind of feeling that everything wasn't quite right. So he hired a private detective.

There in his hands Jon had copies of email messages that had been exchanged between Kurt and Sharron. As I read them I couldn't believe what I was seeing. They were disgusting, filled with details of things they had done together and of things they planned to do. Of course there was other evidence of their affair – dates, times, and places that they had been together.

My world had just been turned upside down. I was in a state of shock. But I didn't question the truth of what was being told to me. In fact, I started thinking of recent behaviors and conversations that should have been a sign – if I had even the slightest thought that Kurt would do something like this to me, which of course I didn't.

Jon was shaking as he told me what he knew. When he learned that I was about to walk down the aisle, he felt I had to know so that I could make a decision with open eyes.

I didn't hesitate. I said, "I have to cancel a wedding. I need to move out of my house." I couldn't believe it was even me talking. How could I possibly cancel all the wonderful plans that I had been making?

As our conversation continued I finally turned to the woman in the back seat and asked, "Who are you?" She introduced herself as Jon's sister. Jon had asked her to be with him, thinking that I might be more comfortable talking with him if he wasn't alone. He had no idea how I'd react. For some reason even that made good sense to me.

I asked if they would drive me around to my office and allow me to make copies of the email messages. I was shaking like a leaf and having trouble functioning – so I only copied a few of the emails and gave them back to Jon. He assured me he would be keeping them and would make them available if at any point I needed them.

We exchanged cell phone numbers before he left. Jon promised that he was going to be calling to make sure I was all right. He was obviously concerned.

Once alone I called my good friend Mike who worked at LaCosta with me. He came running to my office to see what was wrong. I don't think he had ever seen or heard me so upset. I told Mike the story, sobbing as I related everything I had just learned. Mike agreed to cover for me at work – I had a lot to do.

I went to my car and, in a daze, began the drive home. I knew the next call I had to make was to my mother. I couldn't imagine telling her. She would be shocked and she would be worried about me. Bad enough that I had an unfaithful fiancée, but I had a wedding to cancel. A wedding that Mom had worked so hard to make perfect for me, at a price that was well beyond the original budget she had set.

I knew she was even then driving to Vermont and that I couldn't tell her what was happening while she was behind the wheel. I'd ask her to call me when she got to the cottage and I'd tell her then.

I dialed her cell phone and waited as I heard it ring.

Chapter III

PATTY

I picked up my cell phone and saw it was Kyle calling. "Hi Kyle." As always I was anxious to talk with her, especially today as I wanted to share with her the names of the last responses that came in for the wedding and tell her about all the appointments I'd been scheduling to bring the final wedding arrangements together.

I heard the response, "Hi Mom" and instantly knew Kyle was not having a good day. She sounded sad. Maybe she just was not in the mood for work, or maybe she was feeling bad that we would be in Vermont and she wouldn't. She then asked me where I was. "New Jersey," I said. "Why?"

Kyle asked me to call her back when I arrived at the cottage. I wasn't going to wait six hours to find out what had her so down in the dumps so I said, "Kyle what's the matter?" It took some coaxing for her to open up. She didn't want to tell me this news while I was driving. I assured her there was no traffic and I was fine. But I must admit I was not prepared for what I would hear next. In a trembling voice she said, "Mom, we have a wedding to cancel."

If her voice hadn't trembled I would have thought she was joking. Especially since just a few weeks earlier she had been at a party where they'd hired a psychic as part of the entertainment. Kyle had removed her engagement ring – she didn't want to give her any hints! The psychic told her that she did not see a wedding in her near future. I had been in Rome, Italy at the time, and she'd called me there to tell me not to be alarmed but the psychic said there wasn't a wedding coming up. We laughed about it. In fact, I told her that we were having a banquet that same night and had hired fortune tellers as part of *our* entertainment. I would see what they had to say to me. I remember calling her back that night – there definitely is a wedding – the psychic told me that she saw me planning a very successful event. The only event I'd been planning outside of the conference I was at was her wedding!

But I could tell this was no joke. I asked her what she was talking about. Kyle relayed the story to me. I honestly couldn't believe it. Not Kurt. I had no doubt about how much he loved her. This certainly did not sound like the man we knew. I said, "Kyle there are two sides to every story. You need to talk to Kurt and give him the benefit of the doubt". But Kyle was adamant. There was no doubt – she had proof in hand.

She had to go as she was approaching her house, where she planned to pack her belongings and leave as soon as she could. I made her promise that she would call me back as soon as she could, and she agreed. Before hanging up I said, "Kyle, remember – be brave, be strong, be proud. I love you." She responded with "I know Mom, I'll call you later."

And there I was, six hours away from my destination and thousands of miles away from my daughter who was slipping into a despair that I couldn't imagine and one that I couldn't do anything about.

I wanted to be with Kyle, to support her through this, to help her move if that is what she needed to do. I wanted to be there to provide whatever she needed. But, I was here – she was there. I said a prayer that she would be all right. I know that she is a strong young woman, but this had obviously shaken her world.

As I was thinking of Kyle I also began thinking about the fact that we really might have a wedding to cancel. I wasn't ready yet to believe that was true – although Kyle sounded pretty definite on the phone. She might change her mind once she heard Kurt's side of the story.

KYLE

I hung up the phone after talking to Mom. I know she is now driving to Vermont – worried about me. I couldn't help but hear the sadness and disappointment in her voice. But thank God she ended the conversation with those words, "Kyle, remember – be brave, be strong, be proud. I love you." These are words I've heard or read from my mother hundreds of times over the years. Every letter she ever wrote to me once I left home was signed with that closing. I'm not sure how I'll make it through this, but I know that I will.

I pulled into my yard, ran into the house and began packing. I had a beautiful suit case that I had received at my bridal shower – I opened it and began putting everything I could into it. I dragged it out and loaded it into the back end of my Jeep and went back for more of my belongings. The adrenaline was flowing. I found myself lifting things I never normally could have.

I didn't take anything that was "ours" together – only what was clearly mine. I was so upset I could hardly think straight. How could Kurt have done this to me? What had I ever done to deserve this? Hadn't our engagement meant anything to him? The moment I put that ring on my finger I was committed – I thought he had been too!

My sadness was beginning to turn to anger. Without giving it much thought I pulled his clothes from the closet and brought them out onto the lawn – pulled out the hose – and sprayed them into a wet muddy pile. It wouldn't hurt them much, but I thought it would make me feel better. It didn't.

I went back into the house for one last look and as I was leaving Kurt pulled into the yard. How did he know I was there? Evidently "Sharron" had sent him an email letting him know that I had received a visitor at work this morning, since she had been confronted the night before.

He was surprised to see the Jeep loaded and ready to go. "Babe, don't leave me. It isn't true. I've never been with anyone else. I love you. I want to marry you." Blah blah blah was all that I could hear.

"Kurt, save it. I don't believe you. I have details of your meetings. I have emails written back and forth between the two of you. How stupid do you think I am? I have been working overtime and weekends to help us get ahead while you are having an affair with another woman."

He denied it. "Kyle, it looks worse on paper than it really is. I have never even been alone with her."

I could see the panic in his eyes. He was trapped, trying desperately to make me believe that what I had heard was a lie. My heart was wishing he was telling the truth, but my head knew he was not. "Kurt, listen to some of these emails. Now I know that the nights you said you were crashing at your friend's house were really spent sleeping with her. How could you do this to me, to us?"

Within minutes, what began as denials soon turned into True Confessions. He began slowly – we just kissed. He then moved to – we just slept together once.

Then my phone rang. I left him standing there crying and throwing up. I turned away to answer the call. It was my mother checking to see if I was all right. She wanted to know if I had spoken to Kurt. I shared with her that we had just finished our conversation, that he had admitted everything, and that I was moving out. I promised I'd call her back.

When I turned back to Kurt he began begging me to stay. He loved me. He wanted to marry me. Please forgive him. He promised it meant nothing.

But to me it meant everything. How could the man I love cheat on me and just weeks before our wedding? Isn't the most important thing in any marriage trust? What kind of life would we have if this is how we began our marriage? I knew that I couldn't go through with it – no matter what.

I also knew that I didn't deserve this and I wasn't going to be blamed for any of it. I told him that he needed to tell his parents just what he'd done. So I dialed the phone. When his mother answered I said, "Hi Pam, your son has something to tell you." I handed the phone to Kurt.

Kurt took the phone, but he didn't fess up. "Mom, Kyle thinks that I've been unfaithful. It is just a misunderstanding – I love her and would never cheat on her. Right now Kyle is saying she wants to cancel the wedding. He was walking away as he spoke with her – I'm sure he didn't want me to hear his lies. At that point I wasn't sure how many more of his lies I could take. So I did a quick run of the house to see if there was anything else I should take. At that moment none of it seemed too important so I decided it would be best to just get out of there.

Kurt was off the phone and he watched as I got in my Jeep and drove out of the driveway, leaving him alone and crying, watching me drive away.

I had no idea where to go. My friends were all working. I couldn't go back to work. So, I drove to the beach. Being on the water has always helped me think straight and work things out. Hopefully it would help today too. I rolled out my towel and sat down. Alone on the beach I cried. I cried for the love I had just lost, for the hurt I was feeling for having been betrayed, and for the wedding that would never be.

The next call that came was from my girlfriend Sunni. She lives with my friend Mike. She was working and would be with me as soon as she could. She asked me to move in with her and Mike until I figured out what I wanted to do. I thanked her and said that I would.

My mother and I exchanged a few more phone calls, but then she got into an area of the trip that had bad cell service so she promised to call me as soon as she arrived in Vermont.

Actually I was glad for the time alone. I wasn't ready to talk to anyone, including my mother, with whom I normally shared everything. I needed some time to myself to just think before I had to face my friends. I was not only sad, but I was also embarrassed. I felt like such a loser.

Jon called to check on me. I told him that I had left and shared with him the conversation with Kurt. He understood completely. In fact, he was having similar feelings since he had just experienced his own conversation just the day before. When we hung up he ended with, "Kyle, I'm sorry that this has happened but if nothing else at least we each made a new friend." Although not much consolation at the time, it was a nice comment.

Hours later I pulled into Sunni's driveway where I was greeted by hugs and a glass of wine. Together we talked, we cried, and yes – sometimes we even laughed. The laughter I found was a good defense mechanism – it was helping me face the awful truth of what had just happened. I wanted to talk to Mom one more time today too. I knew she'd call when she got to the cottage. I wondered how she would tell Dad. I wondered what Dad would say. I know how much he loves me.

It made me feel sad knowing how awful this was going to make him feel.

I also had a very strong sense of guilt. I was feeling terrible about the disappointment my family would feel, but worse yet, the expenses they were facing which, at least for now, would be for nothing. There would be no wedding to show for the investment they had made in me. Hopefully there would still time to rescue something out of this.

When I finally went to bed that night it was a restless sleep. I went through the last few weeks in my mind – looking for signs I might have missed. Looking for answers to all of my questions, answers that I would never find.

PATTY

The sun was setting as I neared Alburgh. I will be at the cottage in just a few more minutes. Sherwood just called with his usual "Car 54 where are you?" He quickly figured out I wasn't in a laughing mood, as I shared with him Kyle's day. Like me, he didn't believe it. It certainly didn't sound like the Kurt we knew. Perhaps with a new day Kurt would have a chance to share the truth with Kyle – clear up any misunderstandings. Clearly it was all just a bad mistake.

I pulled into the yard right behind my step-daughter Sherri. Her husband David had arrived earlier. I greeted everyone. Sherwood gave me a big hug and Ernie did his "happy dog" dance – he was always so glad to see me! We went into the cottage and I said I had to make a phone call. Kyle was top of mind and she was expecting me to call as soon as I arrived.

I went into our bedroom and closed the door behind me. With Ernie lying across my lap I called Kyle. She shared with me that she was staying with Sunni for awhile. She told me how grateful she was to have such good friends and such a supportive family. I asked her to join us in Vermont and she agreed that she would. The next day she would have Lisa help her book a ticket – it would probably be Sunday before she could make it. Before we hung up I asked her if she would mind me calling Kurt's mom. We agreed that I would make that call in the morning.

But now I had a husband, stepdaughter and stepson waiting in the other room, all anxious to find out what was going on. I sat down with Sherwood and asked him to get Sherri and David. Once we were all together I repeated the events of the day. We all cried.

Sherwood and I were on the exact same page. We weren't concerned over the expense of canceling a wedding – whatever it meant to us we would deal with when the time came. For now, our concern was for our daughter. We wanted to help her heal and we wanted her to be with us.

David and Sherri were so proud of Kyle. Sherri couldn't get over how brave Kyle was. She said if she was in the same situation she probably would go through with the wedding anyway, simply because she wouldn't want anyone to know the truth. Both Sherri and David agreed she didn't need a marriage that was a sham.

After speaking with them, I had to make another important call to Keith and Julia. I knew they would be crushed. They were so close to Kyle. Like us, they questioned the truth of the story – we all knew Kurt and it was so out of character for him. Keith was going to call Kyle. I felt a little better just knowing that as always, he would be there for her. I was so thankful that they had grown not only into a loving brother and sister, but also the best of friends.

Later, after Sherri and David had left, I decided to call my sister Kathy. She lives in Florida and was arriving today at my brother Steve's house just 15 minutes down the road. Maybe she and Steve could come over and talk. I needed a second opinion on what to tell everyone, and when to tell them. Kathy was in the process of organizing the bridal shower for my niece Misty, which was scheduled for the following Saturday. I didn't want Kyle's news to take anything away from Misty. Do I keep this to myself until after, or do I tell people now. I really couldn't imagine sharing the story, but I knew I had to eventually. I called but no one answered. They must have gone out to dinner. I left a message.

It was 9:00 p.m. before my call was returned. Kathy and Dick had gone out to dinner. Steve had been at a golf tournament all day and wasn't home yet. Since it was late I didn't ask her to come over, but we spent a long time talking about everything. As much as I had been dreading it, talking really did help. Kathy told me she thought I needed to tell everyone. We have a large supportive family and people would want to know. It would be too difficult to keep it to myself, and with Kyle coming home we would be faced with having to either avoid everyone or tell them something. I had already tried avoiding phone calls, so I knew her advice was the right thing for me to do. I asked her to tell Steve, who was with my other brother Tom when they got home. I would call the rest of the family in the morning.

I went to bed that night with my own nightmares. I was feeling my daughter's pain and I was mentally making a list of all the planning that would need to be reversed. We had agreed to wait until Monday – not that we really thought anything would change – but we didn't want to act too soon "just in case."

Chapter IV

PATTY

I woke to a beautiful Saturday morning. The sun was shining in the cottage windows and the lake was so still. It was the perfect day, or should have been.

I got my cup of coffee, and with Ernie at my heels joined Sherwood on the screened in porch. Typical of Sherwood he had been ciphering all morning. That is a joke with us. Whenever money is involved he starts figuring out the impact – I would call him Jethro (the nephew on the Beverly Hillbillies). Jethro was good at ciphering too!

The night before I had shared with him my concern over the room block I had contracted at the Basin Harbor Club, guaranteeing 25 rooms. When the responses started coming in and our guests were planning to stay at the resort I had signed amendments that now had us liable for 45 rooms. With no one coming – we would be liable for the full expense.

Sherwood assured me that we would be fine. We could cover the extra room expense by using the home equity line of credit on our house. Not ideal, but it would take care of the additional expense. Plus we were still hopeful that we wouldn't have to pay the full expense of the wedding. I would review the contracts later in the day.

I was more concerned right now with the phone call I was going to make to Kurt's mother. I couldn't be sure how much Kurt had shared with her.

Shaking, I made the call. Quickly into our conversation it was clear the story I heard and the story she heard were not the same. She thanked me for calling and said that she had been on the phone with Kurt all night. He was so upset over this awful misunderstanding. She was confident that they would work it out and all that they probably needed was a good night sleep.

Listening to her I became hopeful. Maybe it wasn't as bad as Kyle had thought. So, I asked Pam if she would share with me exactly what Kurt had told her. She said of course, "Kurt said that he had used poor judgment and that Kyle believes he had been unfaithful", but he assured her that he had never even been alone with the woman in question. They had only been together as part of a group of friends at a bar and at the beach. She continued with, "I know my son and he would never cheat on Kyle – he loves her to death."

I said, "Pam I hope that what he told you is the truth. But I do question it. Kyle has detailed emails and a schedule of events that tell her something much different. You need to call Kurt and tell him that if he loves Kyle and wants to marry her he better get his ass over there and save this relationship, because as far as Kyle is concerned right now, the wedding is off. Today she is buying a ticket to join us in Vermont and she plans to leave California in the morning."

I let Pam know that Kyle was at her girlfriend Sunni's. Before we hung up Pam apologized for Kurt's actions and assured me that this would soon be straightened out. My closing words to her were, "I hope you are right, but Pam – brace yourself – because I think Kurt is lying to you too." We left it that I would call her again the next day.

I called Kyle later in the morning to let her know how the conversation went and let her know that Pam was confident it was all a mistake. Kyle said she was positive that it was not a mistake. She gave me her flight information for the next day, and assured me she'd call later. Her friends were surrounding her with support – Lisa, Sunni, Mike, Adam, Mark – they were all with her. I hung up feeling better knowing she was with good friends.

My next task was to review all of my contracts. I began with the one that was our greatest concern. When I got to the cancellation clause my stomach sank. If the contract was cancelled within 60 days of the event we owed 100% of the guaranteed guest count and 100% of the room block – 45 rooms, Friday and Saturday night, with some blocked for even longer periods of time.

I called the wedding coordinator at The Basin Harbor Club. Beth answered and I shared with her that there was a possibility that the wedding was off. I didn't want to confirm anything until Monday but I wanted her to have an idea of what was going on in Kyle's life. I told Beth we'd like to discuss options – we might want to turn the wedding reception into a charity event. Beth let me know she'd work with me in any way she could. Her concern was also for Kyle at the moment. She told me that waiting another week to make a decision wouldn't have an impact one way or another.

Sherwood and I agreed that we wouldn't burden Kyle with discussions about the expense of the wedding. She had enough going on right now. We'd keep those talks between the two of us.

The first inbound call of the day came from my step-son Doug. He was just checking in to make sure I'd arrived safely and he wanted to talk about his wife Rose and their daughters Danielle and Nicole coming to see us. When he asked the question, "what's new?" he received a shock as I proceeded to tell him about the events of the past couple days.

After that call I started dialing. It would be better to have these calls behind me. So I called my mother, my brother Norm (Misty's dad), my sister Barbara, and my sister Jeanne.

Next I put together my list of all the vendors that I needed to call, and wrote the announcement we would send to all of the people on our wedding list. I spoke with Sherri and she agreed to print them for us. When Monday came I'd be ready to start with the cancellation plans if need be. But for now, there wasn't anything else I could do, so I walked down to the water and sat, looking out over the lake. If I were going to be miserable I might just as well be getting tanned!

KYLE

I woke up to the sound of my telephone ringing – it was Mom. I would really like to let this call go into voicemail, but I can't. I know how concerned she is for me, and I know she wants to make sure that I'm ok.

So I picked up the receiver. "Hi Mom – did you forget there is a three hour time difference?" I knew she hadn't but I had just had the worse night's sleep of my life and I had a pounding headache – so my choice of words reflected how I was feeling.

She responded, "Kyle, I'm so sorry – I just had assumed you would be up. I wanted to tell you about my conversation with Pam." That got my attention – I really did want to know how Kurt's family was reacting to all of this. In the four years we had been together I had grown to love them like my own family.

Mom relayed the conversation with me – I could hear the hope in her voice. "Mom," I said. "Kurt is lying to her. I'm going to call him and tell him that he owes it to his parents to be truthful with them."

I then reassured Mom that I was okay, even though I really wasn't sure that I was. I also let her know that I felt so lucky to have great friends supporting me. We had booked my ticket on-line the night before and I told her I'd call later with my flight details. I'd be coming in on Sunday. I couldn't wait to hang up the phone and bury my head. I think I went to bed hoping I'd wake up in the morning and all of this would just be a bad dream. It was – but I was living it.

I called Kurt's cell phone. When he answered I got to my point immediately. "My mother just got off the phone with your mom. Your mother is going to be calling you soon – when she does you better be honest with her or I'll call her and read some of these emails to her. She won't think you are so innocent then." Kurt tried to talk more, but I had nothing further to say to him at the moment. My headache was getting worse and I really had to throw up again. I'm not good at throwing up but I spent most of the night hugging the toilet bowl. The whole situation literally had made me sick.

Sleep wasn't going to be on my agenda that day. The next thing I knew Kurt was at Sunni's house. I had never told him where I was so I was a little surprised to see him there. I wasn't in the mood for this. I was at least happy to see that he looked as bad as I felt. He began, "Kyle, I love you. We can work this out. I know I've hurt you. I know you don't deserve this. I still want to marry you. What can I do to make you believe me? She means nothing to me, it was just poor judgment. I made a terrible mistake. Please forgive me."

Blah blah blah. How could he possibly think I would ever want him back after he cheated on me this close to our wedding day? Would I have thought a little differently if it had been a one night stand, too much to drink, a stupid mistake. Well we'll never know because it wasn't! Kurt had a relationship. They had been seeing each other for six weeks.

Of all the emails I had read, the one that hurt the most wasn't one describing their sexual encounters. It was the one where they mocked our future marriage. Sharron wrote, "How does Sharron Swanson sound, ha ha." To which Kurt responded, "It rolls right off the tongue!" He was marrying me in a few weeks and telling another woman that her name with his just rolled off the tongue. I would never forgive him.

When he left I think he realized that there was no chance for a future together. He couldn't explain why he had done what he had, and he knew that was the one question I needed an answer to.

I got in the shower hoping that the hot water would relieve the pounding in my head. I wasn't looking forward to getting out and facing my day. But, obviously, I had to. Sunni and Mike had gone to work so I had a few minutes to myself before Lisa arrived. Lisa came with the details of my flight to Vermont. As much as I wanted to be alone my friends weren't going to let me. Thank God for them! They made me talk, they even made me laugh.

There were phone calls that I needed to make. First I had to call work. Mike had covered for me the day before, and told people I had gone home sick. Today I would need to call and let them know what happened and ask for some time off. I needed to be in Vermont. I needed to be with my family. I really, physically, couldn't imagine trying to work right now, not the way I was feeling. My job requires a lot of energy. It's a service-oriented position, and a manager/leader to two teams. I could not pull off the image the company wants to see in its managers. Luckily, when I spoke with them they were wonderful. So understanding and supportive, they wanted me to take whatever time I needed. One burden was lifted.

My next calls were to the other two women I had asked to be in my wedding. Jess was going to be my Matron of Honor. I had known her since we lived in St. John years earlier. When I moved to California, Kurt and I lived with Jess, her husband Gabe and their son until we got our own place. As I dialed her number I remembered that when we first got there Jess did not like Kurt. She didn't feel he was right for me – but with time he had won her over. After all, if I had chosen him, he must be all right.

Jess was shocked with the story. She couldn't believe that Kurt would have ever cheated on me. However, she did tell me that maybe it was for the best – she thought I could do better. And, like everyone else, thank God I found out before I married him. I knew that Jess would be supportive. She was such a good friend, just weeks earlier she had flown to Vermont to be a part of my bridal shower. We stayed at the lake cottage with Mom and Dad. She felt like part of my family. She was going to come down to be with me. I told her how much I appreciated the thought, but really, she did not need to. I was going home the next day. So we agreed to stay in touch.

Ann was my other bridesmaid. I had met Ann in St. John too, and then we'd reconnected when I moved from St. John to Charleston, South Carolina where she now lived. Ann was the person who introduced me to Kurt. One evening, Ann and I had gone out for a drink – as we were sitting there visiting over a glass of wine this guy came in that just took my breath away. Ann had arranged for us to meet – she thought we would be perfect for each other. He certainly had a look I loved - he was tall, with black curly hair, and beautiful blue eyes. At that moment his outfit was even adorable - he was wearing fisherman's rubber bib overalls! My heart flipped and I think it truly was love at first sight. Within six months I'd be bringing him to Vermont on vacation to meet my parents for the first time. Then the future looked bright – not so much so now!

I had spoken with my brother Keith and sister-in-law Julia the evening before. Now they were calling again. The night before I know they had been at a loss for words. Keith wanted to know how I was doing today and he wanted to make sure I was going to come home. I assured him that I was, and then asked if he would pick me up at the airport. I really needed to see him. He promised he would come and get me, and he told me he would tell Mom. I didn't want to hurt her feelings, but it was Keith I wanted to see first.

My friend Adam showed up at lunch time with pizza and beer. I couldn't even think of eating, and I had no desire to have a beer. But, here was one of my best guy friends supporting me the best he knew how – and I was touched. Adam and I have been through a lot together. We've been friends since college. I was with him when he learned his father died. News like that creates a bond that will keep us close for the rest of our lives. After college we stayed in touch. He came to visit me in St. John for a week, and the week turned into six months. After that he left for California where he was going to teach kindergarten, which is what we'd both gone to school for in the first place. It was Adam who encouraged me to follow my dream and come out to California.

So for Adam's (and old time's) sake, I ate a piece of pizza and told him about all that had happened over the last two days.

It was during my visit with Adam that I realized I couldn't walk away without having one more conversation with Kurt. I so wanted to know why – how – Kurt could have done this to me. I also needed to let him know that there would be no chance of reconciliation. I was definitely going to cancel the wedding.

I called Kurt and scheduled a meeting for early that evening.

We met at our apartment. It was painful going back there, to our house, a place where we had shared so much together. We had been so excited when we found the apartment. Prior to that we'd been living with two of my friends – Adam and Mark – but once we got engaged we decided we needed our own space. This apartment was just one block away and very close to the beach so it would be easy for Kurt to go surfing, a passion of his, and for me to just bask in the sun, a passion of mine. It was small but affordable. Perfect for what we needed at the time.

The meeting was difficult. I had to approach it with my defenses up. I had already been hurt enough by him. He started the conversation by apologizing and telling me how much he loved me. I listened, but what I didn't hear was the why. I told him my reason for meeting with him was to make sure he realized we were done, the wedding was off, and that I was going to Vermont to be with my family. Once I got there we would begin cancelling all of our plans. He needed to start letting his friends and family know. I also needed him to promise that they would know the reason our plans were being cancelled. I did not want them to think I was responsible – clearly it was not my choice to gamble my future away on a meaningless relationship.

It was time for Kurt to be a man and step up to what he had done. He agreed. I also let him know how unfair I thought this was to my parents. Did he realize that they would be on the hook for the full expense of the wedding yet would have nothing to show for it? I wanted him to realize that his actions would have far more than just an emotional impact. He had created a financial hardship too. He acknowledged this and I knew when he said how sorry he was about that, he was telling the truth. I know he loved my family and had been looking forward to being a part of it. He had already started calling my mother Mom. He also told me that if there was anything from our pre-paid honeymoon that could be rescued that he wanted that to go towards the wedding expense. We would later learn that the honeymoon package had also been non-refundable, and, not anticipating any problems, we had not taken out any travelers insurance. So it either needed to be used or it too would be lost.

I hugged him when I left, but I was numb. I felt nothing but sorrow. Sadness for what we could have had together. I also realized then that I would never be able to have him touch me again. He was no longer the man I had been in love with.

Later my friends drove me to the airport so I could take the red eye back East. I was going home.

Chapter V

PATTY

I was so glad to be at the lake. I couldn't imagine being anywhere else right now. I was lying in a lounge chair on the dock reflecting on the events of the last 24 hours. What a difference a day makes. Yesterday I got in my car heading for Vermont with the excitement of a much-needed vacation, a wedding to plan, and best of all, family time. I was especially looking forward to seeing our granddaughter McKenna – she's just six months old now and growing so fast. And then of course there was Misty's bridal shower, my trip to California for a short business meeting, and Kyle's second bridal shower.

Today my heart was aching for Kyle. The changes in her life made my own pale in comparison. She woke up yesterday in love, making plans for the wedding of her dreams. She went to bed with a broken heart. Today she has a broken engagement, a cancelled wedding, and a ticket home to Vermont. What a sad turn of events.

Being on the water has always been good medicine for Kyle. Hopefully being here with family will be good for her. I asked her to spend at least one week, and play it by ear after that. She agreed.

Later that morning, Sherwood came to join me on the dock. He made a lunch. He is probably one of the nicest men in the world. As we sat together we didn't talk much, but just being together seemed to help the both of us. He was monitoring phone calls for me. The only ones I wanted to take were family calls.

My sister Kathy came over for a few minutes – just to give me support. It was so appreciated!

My sister Barbara and her family came over later in the day. They have a home on the lake just 10 minutes away. They brought a bottle of wine and we sat at the water visiting. Barbara and Kyle have always been close. Growing up, Barbara was the youngest of my sisters and was Kyle's babysitter, and later her friend. They are a lot alike. Barbara assured me that Kyle was a strong woman – like her mother – and she would get through this. I knew she was right, but hearing someone else say it helped!

That evening I called Kurt's mother back. I knew when I heard her voice that Kurt had finally told her the truth. She shared their conversation with me and she sobbed throughout the call. She was so sorry for what he'd done to Kyle, she was so sorry for what he'd done to us, she was so sorry for what he'd done to them, but most of all she was so sorry for what he did to himself. She had never heard him sound so sorrowful. As bad as it was, and as wrong as he had been, he was her son and she was feeling his pain. As much as we tried not to – Keith, Julia, Sherwood and I, were all feeling bad for him too. But also mad – and sad for Kyle. It was quite a mix of emotions.

Pam wanted to assure me that she and Jim would help make this right. I assumed she meant financially since there was nothing much else they could do. But I told her we had plenty of time to talk about that later, right now we both needed to worry about helping our children through this. I could tell she was thankful for my position on this. She was going to fly out in a few days to be with Kurt. We agreed to stay in touch.

I went to bed again that night exhausted and full of sadness. I couldn't wait to see Kyle. I needed to give her a hug. I don't know why but I was sure that if I hugged her hard enough I could absorb some of her pain. That was a crazy thought – but it helped me to think I had that kind of power.

KYLE

I checked in for my flight feeling like a zombie. I was going through all of the necessary motions to get me where I needed to be, but my head just wasn't in it. As I stood in line to board the plane a woman looked at me and said, "You look like you've just received some bad news." What a bazaar thing to say to someone you don't know, but the gesture set me off and I began to sob. Like the parting of the seas, everyone stepped aside as they moved me to the front of the line.

I was exhausted from all I'd been through and the lack of sleep from the nights before. With the help of a valium I planned to sleep for this whole flight. Fortunately there were some empty rows, I chose one and did exactly that. I slept for the next five hours. My connection was in Philadelphia with a short lay over. But to my surprise, the connecting flight was on schedule – unusual for Philadelphia. I called Keith to let him know exactly when I thought we'd be landing and he promised he'd be waiting for me.

True to his word as I came through the gates, he was right there. I ran to him, and in the middle of the airport I sobbed uncontrollably. He just held me. I am so blessed to have Keith as my brother. Once I was able to get my emotions in check he took my hand and held tight, clearly making me feel like the protected little sister. We went to the car to join Julia and McKenna for our ride to the cottage.

As much as I wanted to see my parents, I was dreading it. I felt so sad, for me and for them. I felt guilty that I was costing them a lot of money for nothing. I knew that they would never bring that up as an issue – but I felt terrible about it just the same.

As we drove in the yard Dad and Ernie were there to meet us. Ernie did his happy dance, and Dad hugged me and told me that he loved me.

I then went to the cottage and Mom met me at the door. She hugged me so hard! I cried again. Keith, Julia and McKenna stayed outside for awhile so that I could have some time alone with Mom and Dad. My parent's eyes were filled with love, sadness and concern. I knew they were feeling awful for me. But, I know Mom – she won't be able to play that role for too long. She will still feel sorry for me but she will want to talk about moving forward and keeping positive. She likes to have a plan! She also believes that life is what you make it, so she'll want to start talking about what we want to make of this.

To my surprise she didn't start heading in that direction on my first day back. We sat together as a family and talked about everything that had happened. Then Mom and I went to sit by the water. If we are going to be sad, we might as well be getting tanned!

(And no, that's not a family philosophy!)

Mom told me that my aunts and my grandmother would all be at my sister Barbara's house the next day, if I felt up to going. I thought it would be a good idea. I knew I would have to face people sometime and being with my Nana and my Aunts would be the best place for me to start. I knew that they would be supportive but not smothering, and I also knew they would make me laugh. That's just what happens when the Burrington's get together.

But thankfully, on that first day, it was just Mom, Dad, Keith, Julia, McKenna and Me. Dad kept trying to get me to eat, in just these few days I had lost weight and I was already thin enough – so he would do his part not to let me lose anymore! Having McKenna with us changed the focus from my problems to her. She was such a welcome addition to the family and Keith and Julia are such great parents. It was fun to see them in this new role. Mom was Mom – as usual she was just there for me. When I wanted to talk she would listen, when I wanted to just sit there we'd sit there. But she's also very funny and when we did talk we would find little things to laugh about. As heavy as my heart was, it did seem a little lighter just being around family.

The weather was beautiful – the sun was shining bright on the lake. I would shut my eyes to soak up the sun's rays and the visuals of the last few days would come rushing through my mind. Oh how I wish I could forget quickly about all that happened and move on – but at this moment I didn't feel like that would ever happen.

In our conversation of what happened, Keith, Julia, Mom and Dad all had questions about Jon; they wanted to know who this man was that came to tell me the news. I shared with them what I could; but honestly, I didn't know that much about him. We had shared several phone calls by now – but all were focused on how we each were doing. Although my family was of course concerned for me, Jon was experiencing similar feelings. He wasn't cancelling a wedding but he was ending a five year relationship that he had thought would be leading to more. We were going to help each other through this. We even made a vow that when we were ready we would be each other's first date.

Now, I found it hard to describe him to my family. I could only remember a tall, dark, attractive man. His features were foggy to me. I hoped I would recognize him when I finally did see him again in person. My family was positioning him as a hero – if it hadn't been for him

I would be walking down the aisle to who knows what. He definitely saved me from making a big mistake.

Keith made dinner for us that night. It was amazing. To my own surprise I ate nearly all of it. He had also brought some great wines. Mom cleaned up so that Keith, Julia and I could go watch the sunset and have some time to visit among ourselves. Keith wanted me to call Mike – my biological father. I'm sorry to say that unlike Keith, I really don't have much of a relationship with him, and frankly was feeling like he represented everything I was trying to forget about. For Keith, I would call him later.

The sunset that evening was amazing and reminded me how beautiful nature can be. But for me, the night just brought more sadness. Kurt never made it to the cottage. He will never see the sunset from this spot. I will never share with him all that we had planned. But tomorrow the sun will rise again and hopefully I'll feel better with each new day.

I went to bed feeling completely worn out again. But sleep did not come easy. I tossed and turned all night long. When I heard Dad making coffee in the morning I was quick to get up and join him. We sat on the porch, drank coffee, and had our own quiet visit. To my surprise he also encouraged me to call Mike. I'm not sure why it should have surprised me. Dad had made sure we had included Mike and his wife in everything growing up from birthday parties to Christmas dinners.

I told Dad how grateful I was for him and Mom. I also let him know that I appreciated Sherri's support. That is when he cried for the first time in front of me. He loves all of his children so much and his wish has always been that we will stay close. I assured him that we will.

As always, it was nice having some private time with Dad. It was important for me to let him know how much I loved him and how much his support meant to me. He was always so giving. Mom joined us a little later, and of course, Ernie was right behind her.

We talked about going out to dinner later in the week, and we selected the restaurant we'd try. We had heard good things about the North Hero House; Mom would make reservations for Wednesday. At that moment going out to dinner was one of the last things I felt like doing, but I knew they thought it would do me well, so I agreed.

Keith, Julia and McKenna left for home early that morning. Keith had a lot to do at the restaurant he and Julia own, near the Sugarbush ski area. They promised they'd keep in touch, and would be back up over the weekend.

Mom and I got ready to go to Aunt Barbara's – she gets the morning sun! I knew that my Nana, Aunt Kathy and Aunt Jeanne would be there too. I might as well face my reality head on and start telling people what had happened. I know they'll be uncomfortable too.

Dad was going to join us a little later in the day.

It was much easier than I had expected. I got the hug and kiss from each of them as I had expected. We then lined our lounge chairs up across the water's edge and began talking. I told them my story, I answered their questions, and true to Burrington form, they had me laughing in no time. Again, everyone had a lot of questions about Jon. My family believes in fate, and everyone was sure that Jon was sent to me for a reason…I think they are all hoping it will be more than just to let me know I had a cheating fiancé. I truly doubt that, but right now he was being a good friend – continuing to check on me to make sure I was doing ok. I appreciated that.

It was a great day, all things considered. We played in the water, we ate, we had drinks, we talked, and we laughed. In our conversations we approached the subject of what we could do at the Basin Harbor Club in place of a wedding reception. Mom mentioned a charity event, we talked about a family party, but at the moment I couldn't face doing anything there. Although it did seem a shame not to benefit from the investment my parents were making. Maybe there would be something they could do that didn't involve me.

I called my cousin Misty when I got back to the cottage. I wanted to have a conversation with her. It was important for me to let her know that this was my problem and it would pass. I didn't want it to impact her bridal shower that was now just days away, and certainly not her wedding! Growing up, Misty was much more than a cousin to me. We were close in age, and we were really best friends. I loved her and wanted nothing but happiness for her.

Misty and her fiancée, Chris, were going to be staying at the cottage the night of her shower. Mom had planned a dinner for them. We still wanted that to happen. I wouldn't be able to be at the shower, but I definitely would be there when they came to the cottage. We would talk more then.

Sherri stopped by with the printed cancellation notices. We were ready to move on.

That night for the first time in days, I actually slept.

PATTY

I got up early the morning after Kyle arrived. Finally I had a good night's sleep. I was prepared to start cancelling the wedding!

I started making the calls. By the time Kyle got up I had cancelled the Vermont Symphony Orchestra, the band, the flowers, the photographer, and the Justice of the Peace.

Without hesitation she sat down and together we addressed all the notices. It was clear she was committed to her decision. Sherwood took them to the post office – we were officially cancelled.

It was time to call Pam again. Pam told me she was going to California to be with Kurt. She was worried about him. She had never heard him sound so down. I think she was afraid he would do something to himself. I personally doubted that.

Pam continued to apologize for Kurt's behavior, and when she returned from California she wanted to talk about what they could do to help financially. I again told her that that discussion could wait, and that I didn't feel it was their responsibility to help. I told her I felt it was up to Kurt to make things right. The real reason for my call was to let her know we had sent out the wedding cancellation notices, and that they had gone to everyone on the invitation list. The message was simple, "It is with deep regret and heavy hearts that the Paxman/Swanson wedding has been cancelled." Sincerely, Sherwood and Patty Carbee

Kyle walked into the room just as Pam was asking about her. Kyle knew that it was Pam on the phone and she signaled to me that she would like to talk to her. So, I asked Pam if she'd like to speak to Kyle. Of course she did.

KYLE

I was nervous about talking with Pam. I didn't know how it would make me feel. I took the phone out onto the back deck and the conversation began with both of us sobbing.

Pam apologized for Kurt. She told me how much her whole family loved me. She said she prayed that we would find a way to get back together. I assured her that would never happen. I then told her some of the story from my perspective, and without going into the disgusting details I let her know the depth of the emails I read. I asked her how he could have done something like this to me, especially six weeks before our wedding. She assured me that it was bad judgment. She said it had started as just flirting and then got out of control. She felt there was no explanation that would ease my pain.

The one thing I wanted her to know is that I expected her to let her side of the family know what had happened. I did not want any of them thinking this was in any way my fault. I wanted the responsibility to clearly lie with Kurt. She agreed. When we hung up we promised to stay in touch. But deep down I knew that I would probably never speak with her again. I would have to make this a clean break.

My friends, my family, and Jon all called throughout the day. It seemed strange that the only call that truly helped me feel better was the one from Jon. Although we didn't know each other well, we were both experiencing the pain that comes from losing someone. It felt good to have him tell me he was proud of me and impressed by the way I was handling myself. Each time we hung up we agreed to stay in touch… it was good therapy!

With another day under my belt I was ready for a night out. Not that I was hungry, but a change of atmosphere would be good.

Mom, Dad and I went to the North Hero House. We got a table by the window on the porch. Over a cocktail Mom began to talk more about the idea of a charity event. I knew I could never get behind having a "party" but a charity event, something that others would benefit from, suddenly was sounding appealing. Mom said that she thought healing would begin when we could turn our thoughts to others. I liked that idea! So the brainstorming began and that is how we spent our evening out.

My mother had been on the board of directors of a non-profit before and with her marketing experience I knew we would be able to make it work, *if* I could get my heart into it.

By the time we got back to the cottage we had pretty much decided that we would have a charity event. We would give tickets away – but the expectation would be made clear up-front that the price of attending would be a donation to one of two charities. We didn't know what charities we'd select but we did know that we would want people to have a choice. We also didn't know where we'd have the event. We could go to the Basin Harbor Club, or we could have it at Keith and Julia's restaurant, The Common Man. The Basin Harbor Club gave a gracious offer – if we decided not to do anything there they would give us the food and we could have our event somewhere else. We would call Keith in the morning to pass the idea by him.

When we got back that night we all went to bed feeling a little better, knowing that our thoughts were now moving in a positive direction.

PATTY

I was so happy when Kyle agreed to consider the charity event. Not that this would save us any money, but at least the money we were spending would not be just thrown away. I was most excited about having something positive for Kyle to focus on. She would have to get 100% behind whatever we decided to do.

When morning came we started making phone calls. The first was to Keith. I told him about our charity event idea and asked him if he would want it at the restaurant. I was surprised when he didn't jump on the idea. He loved the charity twist, but he felt we should have it at the Basin Harbor Club. He pointed out several facts that all made good sense: we were already paying for a cocktail reception, dinner, and five hours of open bar, plus the wait staff. He also felt that the charities would benefit, since this would be demonstrating great strength on

Kyle's part. She'd be hosting an event on what would have been her wedding day at the place she would have been celebrating her future.

He had great points, but it would be a lot more difficult for Kyle – frankly, for all of us.

Kyle would need to think this through. But in the meantime we all agreed that we would move forward with the concept and begin considering which charities we wanted to support.

Of course we had several that were important to us. I had been on the board of directors for the March of Dimes for years. I have a nephew with Cerebral Palsy, a great nephew has autism, we have many people close to us that have been lost to cancer, and we have seen people we love suffer from Alzheimer's. But Kyle wanted to do more research. She felt we were actively supporting these causes already. She wanted to find charities that connected to her.

I love the fact that Kyle doesn't just jump at ideas without giving them serious thought. She wanted to find passion in this event. She wanted to find charities that meant something special to her. So we began listing what was most important to her – our list included family, children, strength, Vermont, women, and adoption.

Later in the day Barbara came by with information on many Vermont-based organizations. One jumped out at us: The Vermont Children's Aid Society. Their mission, "dedicated to the provision of services which seek to support and strengthen families, and promote safe, stable and nurturing environments for children" sounded perfect to us. They offer child and family counseling, pregnancy counseling, adoption planning, lifetime adoption services, post adoption counseling, and more. It was exactly what Kyle had been looking for. Her first charity was selected.

The next morning we were having coffee and visiting. The television was on in the background, which was unusual for us. Suddenly we stopped talking – we were both drawn to a commercial that was playing. It was for CARE. We saw women from around the world gathered together, arms raised in the air, and we heard the saying, "she has the power to change the world, you have the power to help her do it." Without speaking we looked at each other and put our arms in the air too.

Kyle began to cry, and said, "We have found our second cause!"

With that – we also found our theme. Women make a difference. We decided at that moment that our invitation list would include women only – strong charitably minded women. This charity event would make a difference, to the charities we selected and to the people that attended.

Chapter VI

KYLE

It was hard to believe how far our idea had come in just a day. Once my mother sets a goal not much stops her from moving forward. Thankfully, she wasn't doing anything without my buy-in.

The most difficult decision for me was where to hold the event. But after speaking with Keith, I knew he was right. We would have the best results if I could bring myself to host it on the scheduled date, at the scheduled place where my wedding would have been. So as difficult as that might be, I asked Mom to call The Basin Harbor Club and let them know we would be keeping our plans – only the function would change. Now she was busy writing the invitations and contacting my Aunts to see if they would help us distribute tickets. We wanted to give the tickets to strong, charitably minded women.

I was so happy with the two charities I had chosen. Now I needed to contact both of them to see if they were interested in working with us.

The Vermont Children's Aid Society was easy enough to find. We were in Vermont so it was listed in the local phone book. I called and was transferred to their executive director – Steve Habif. I think we shocked him! In the history of the VCAS no one had ever called wanting to host an event that would cost them nothing and help them raise donations. He was wonderful to speak with and so appreciative that we had selected their organization. I asked to have representation from his organization that evening and that I would like someone to speak at the event to help educate our guests. He agreed and I let him know that I'd keep him in the loop as our planning progressed.

Steve's excitement was contagious and really helped me feel great about my decision. Already I could feel the benefit of focusing on others!

I then called information and got phone numbers for CARE. They had offices in New York and Atlanta. After several attempts I ended up speaking with Bibianna Betancourt. The conversation was very much like the one I had earlier with the Vermont Children's Aid Society. She was ecstatic. They definitely wanted to participate and would send me more information on the charity.

Now we had our date, our time, our location, our charities, and Mom shared with me the invitation she had written – she wanted to make sure I approved before she had it printed.

The invitation told the story – like her, it was direct:

Women Make a Difference

A young woman, whose name is Kyle, can light up a room with her glowing smile. She was deep in the midst of making wedding plans when she learned her love was wasted on a cheating man.

The wedding has been cancelled, but the day will not be lost to sadness and sorrow, for this strong woman needs to look forward to her future and each new tomorrow.

We believe healing begins when your thoughts turn to others. So, we are making a plea to friends, sisters, daughters and mothers…

Please join us for a charity event – an event for women, women of strength.

September 9, 2006

The Basin harbor Club

Vergennes, Vermont

Cocktails – 5:00 pm; Dinner – 6:00 pm

Hosted by: Kyle Paxman

Her Mother: Patty Carbee

Her Sisters: Julia Paxman, Sherri Gilmore and Rose Dulac

Her Aunts: Kathleen Tucker, Jeanne Hommel, Barbara Burrington, Laurie Burrington, Diane Burrington, and Michelle Burrington

Her Grandmother: Winnie Burrington

The charities are: CARE and Vermont Children's Aid Society

She also had the tickets written. Once I read and approved them she was off to the store to buy the paper stock. She called my sister Sherri, who was going to get them printed. We were on our way and there was no turning back!

PATTY

It felt good to have a project to focus on. Kyle wasn't the only one that needed something positive.

I was dreading the next day. We had a bridal shower for my niece Misty. I love Misty and was so happy for her. But I wasn't feeling much like celebrating. My goal would be to hold it together and not let anyone know how sad I was personally feeling. Following the shower I had planned a celebration dinner at the cottage for my niece and her fiancée, my sister Kathy and her husband Dick, and my brother Steve and his wife Michelle. Plus Keith, Julia and McKenna were going to come up since their restaurant is closed on Sunday's and Monday's.

Kyle made the right decision. She was not going to attend the shower, but she would of course be joining us for the dinner later that evening. She really was happy for Misty and wanted to make sure that Misty and Chris knew that.

While I'm at the shower she will be busy. First, she has a massage scheduled, then Sherri is going to come up and hang at the water with her, and later in the afternoon her cousin Scott (my sister Jeanne's son) is coming to see her. Hopefully all of this will be good for her!

Scott had experienced a situation several years earlier that was quite similar to Kyle's. Scott is a very private person and had not personally talked about this with anyone, but he called Kyle when he heard her news – he shared her pain and for the first time, his story. I know the afternoon with him will be good for her – and for him.

As I'm driving to the shower my heart is in my stomach. I have a headache. Think positive - I love the gifts I bought and I'll be with family. I know I can get through this. I just need to act happy!

The theme of the shower is a tea party. So I put on my tea party hat and walked into the shower. I was early so most guests weren't here yet – thankfully. I did the customary hugs, I could see the look of "sorry" in everyone's eyes…I kept telling myself, "just keep on laughing Patty, you'll get through this!" I went back to the car to retrieve my presents, and get a needed breath of fresh air. This was going to be more difficult than I thought!

Misty looked so cute, as did everyone else in their bonnets and beads! Even McKenna came with a bonnet on. Thankfully Julia and McKenna sat at my table, and as only a baby can do – McKenna helped me make it through the shower!

As the party ended I gave Misty directions to the cottage, bid farewell to family and friends, and headed back to the lake. I was looking forward to the 45 minute ride alone!

When I got back I would be ready to have a drink and focus on making a dinner.

The night turned out great. We enjoyed cocktails, dinner and conversation. But, I must admit, I was ready for the day to end. Scott, Misty and Chris were all staying over – as of course were Kyle, Keith, Julia and McKenna! I went to bed listening to them all laughing and reminiscing on the porch.

Tomorrow was Sunday and there were no plans. We were all just going to enjoy the water, and each other. Kyle was scheduled to leave on Monday.

KYLE

Saturday was busy, and surprisingly enjoyable!

In the morning I went for a 90 minute massage. I needed that more than I realized. I could feel the tension in my body dissolving. It was wonderful.

When I returned to the cottage Mom had left for Misty's bridal shower. Thank heavens I wasn't going to that. I actually felt bad that Mom had to go, but I know she wouldn't miss it, no matter what.

Sherri had arrived, and was sitting with Dad on the porch. As soon as I got there we put our suits on and headed for the water. Our plan was to spend the day floating on the water, and Dad was going to be our waiter. You can't beat that!!!

It was nice to have that private time with Sherri. She had been so supportive. I really appreciated all she had done. We had great conversation, and she shared with me how proud of me she was. She didn't think that she would have had the strength to handle the situation the same way. I told her I didn't feel I had a choice. There was no other option I would have considered. I asked Sherri if she would participate in the Charity Event as one of the emcees. She was touched, and of course agreed.

Sherri left in the early afternoon and Scott arrived. Timing was perfect! Not wanting to miss any of the fabulous sun, we spent the remainder of the afternoon down at the dock, drinking beers and talking. We really did have similar experiences. In the end I think I helped Scott as much as he helped me.

When Mom got home, and then others arrived, I was ready to see them. It was great to see Misty. I was so happy for her, and needed to let her know that nothing that happened to me should affect her happiness. We would make sure it didn't.

Dinner was fun, and with my mother's family there, full of laughs! It was a good day. I was already dreading returning to San Diego on Monday. I didn't know why, but I really felt I needed at least one more day. I would talk to Mom about it in the morning.

Over coffee the next morning I asked Mom about delaying my flight. She was all for it. I know that she hated to see me leave. I could see how worried she was for me, although she stayed focused on the positive. Always talking about the future – that's Mom!

We called the airline and rescheduled for Tuesday morning, a 6:00 a.m. flight, which would mean leaving the cottage at 4:00 a.m. – ugh.

That evening I asked Mom if she would go on my honeymoon with me! We had prepaid for a ten day trip to Tahiti which would also be lost if we didn't use it. Although I had friends that would love to join me, it was Mom I wanted to be with. She would understand my moods, she would make me laugh, she would be fun – and she'd never been to Tahiti either.

I could tell Mom was happy to be asked, but she wouldn't commit. She didn't have a lot of vacation time left at work. But laughingly she said if her conference call didn't go well the next day, and she lost her job over it, she'd go with me.

PATTY

I am so happy that Kyle is going to stay a day longer. I have a conference call with my boss on Monday morning, but we can spend the rest of the day finalizing details of her charity event. When she goes home I want her to know that everything is taken care of, and although she has the difficulty of facing her friends and colleagues at work she will have a positive twist to add to her story. She has taken lemons and turned it to lemonade. I am so proud of how she is handling herself. She is a strong woman.

At the end of the day on Sunday our guests had left and it was just immediate family again. Although having so much company was a good distraction – sometimes less is more!

Sunday night I went to bed exhausted and frankly dreading my Monday morning conference call. I had kept my staff at work informed of all that was going on with Kyle. I didn't have a choice since I had needed to cancel the short trip to San Diego that had included a business meeting. I realized that if my boss was having a conference call with me while I was on vacation, it must be important. We had been working on strategy, so perhaps he had set a date to communicate the impact. I assumed he wanted to tell me what changes had been agreed to. Or better yet, maybe he just wanted to tell me how well the off-site Executive Team meeting had been and how helpful the information I had put together for him was.

In the morning over breakfast I felt compelled to warn my family that the conversation could go one of two ways. He would either be telling me what is changing and what my new role is, or he'll be telling me about changes and letting me know that I'm not a part of the new strategy -- although I didn't really think the second scenario would be the likely discussion. After all, in the history of the company I had never known them to eliminate anyone's position over the phone.

At 8:30, right on schedule, the phone rang. I took the call in my bedroom. I was ready with phone in hand, paper and pencil. I was prepared to take notes.

Peter began the conversation asking me if I was enjoying my vacation. I thought that was a strange first question since by now he had to know what my family had been dealing with for the past week. But as usual not feeling any of the warm and fuzzy I told him it has been fine.

56

Then the real conversation began. Peter said, "As you know we have been spending months developing our new distribution strategy. Today we are going to be announcing the strategy to the company, and of course prior to making any announcements I want to let you know about the changes and the impact to you."

The tone of his voice was setting the stage for the conversation I had been dreading. I simply replied, "OK". And he continued, "We will be changing our distribution focus and will begin building a strong wholesale division. As a result your position is being eliminated effective immediately." I felt my stomach do a flip, as our conversation continued.

Peter assured me that this decision in no way was a reflection of my skills, ability or performance. My position was being eliminated because he needed to restructure to support the new strategy and he needed the budget dollars that my position represented. He then shared with me "the package." I would get nine months compensation and benefits, and one year's salary bonus. A package was going to be delivered to me overnight.

I asked about some of the other changes, hoping that hearing the whole picture would help me understand his reasoning. Some of the changes made sense to me, others clearly did not. But it really didn't make much difference what I thought at this point.

I actually could have laughed at Peter's closing line. "I know a lot of people in the industry and I'd be glad to help you in any way that I can." I could only respond with, "Thanks." I really just wanted to say, "Yah, right." There was no way that I would ever ask or want help from him in getting my next job. I personally never liked, trusted, or respected him – and now more than ever that was true!

As I hung up the phone I began thinking about my next conversation. I now had to tell my family. Keith, Kyle and Julia were on the porch, but

Sherwood was outside. You could see they were all anxiously waiting to hear about my call. Trying to make it light I said, "Well it looks like I'm going to Tahiti!" With shock on all their faces I continued, "I just lost my job – my position has been eliminated!" I could deal with their shock, but I wouldn't be able to deal with having them be disappointed in me.

Before I went on with my story I asked Keith to go get Dad, I only wanted to tell this story once.

When Sherwood and Keith were back I replayed the conversation with Peter. Then I realized, I had taught them well. They ALL began telling me what a great opportunity this was, and how much happier I'd be, and now I could live wherever I wanted.

We sat there for over an hour discussing this, but then the phone began to ring. Today calls were not coming in to talk about Kyle's situation. Today the calls that were coming in were from my staff, agents, field managers, industry associates and friends. But I had calls I needed to make too. I had to call all of my family again, this time with my news. I had hoped that I would have another three to five years with the company, but that wasn't to be. I was embarrassed that they didn't feel my position was critical to their future success. Now I had to tell others as much.

The best call was to my mother. I could not believe how happy she was! She actually screamed she was so excited, and then she told me that her prayers had been answered. I could come back to Vermont! Although that isn't a decision we had made yet, it certainly was a possibility. The following calls to my step children, to my brothers and sisters, were quite similar. Everyone was happy – evidently they had all missed having us close and hoped that this would get us back.

The calls that came in from those I had worked with were quite different. They were all very upset, and sad that I wasn't going to still be with the company. In fact, the funny part was that although I was the one that had just received the bad news, it was me trying to make them feel better about it.

When I was asked what I was going to do, the answer was easy. "Right now," I told everyone, "I'm going to enjoy the rest of my vacation and plan a great charity event for Kyle. That's it. I need to process the rest and I'm not going to jump into any decisions."

I'm not sure if what had just happened to me helped, or hurt, Kyle's healing process. But it certainly gave all of us something different to talk about for awhile! My last day with Kyle flew by. I spent a lot of time on the phone, but let a lot of calls go directly to the answering machine too. I wanted to enjoy my kids and the lake. So that is how my Monday went!

Keith, Julia and McKenna went home in the early afternoon. Kyle, Sherwood and I enjoyed some quiet time with a nice dinner, and drinks. In the morning Kyle would be leaving for California and she would have to face all that she left behind. I encouraged her to take one more day off from work when she got back to get her stuff together and to settle down.

My head was spinning when I went to bed that night. Now I not only have a cancelled wedding and charity event to plan for Kyle, but I'm unemployed. What a difference a day makes!

Chapter VII

KYLE

I'm nervously waiting for Mom to finish her conference call. I don't know what is going to happen, but I have a feeling this might be why I had a sense that my trip needed to be extended.

When Mom joined us on the porch and I hear her words, "Well it looks like I'm going to Tahiti. I just lost my job – my position has been eliminated!" I knew I had been given one more day in Vermont to help her through this.

It was obvious she wasn't sure what she was feeling, sorry that she lost her job, or happy that she no longer had to work with *Peter*. But when we asked her what she was going to do now she was quick to respond, "Right now I'm going to enjoy the rest of my vacation and plan a great charity event for Kyle. I'm also going to buy my ticket to Tahiti and take a great trip!"

Quickly she moved from her own situation to mine. She really did want to focus on creating a great charity event. And now, more than ever, I wanted to make sure it was great too, as much for Mom as for me.

I really was seeing first hand my mother practice exactly what she has preached for all these years. She was being so brave, so strong, and so proud. She didn't shed any tears for herself and she didn't feel sorry for herself. She just started focusing on the positive.

Later in the day, after Keith and Julia left, we began writing our speeches for the charity event. We planned that Julia would be the emcee for the first half of the program, she would introduce Mom, Mom would give the first speech, and then she would introduce me. I would give my speech and end with a toast to everyone that was there participating in my charity event. We talked through what we wanted to say, Mom took notes, and during the next week she would write our speeches and send me copies to review and edit.

I wished there had been more I could do to help my mother with all that she was going through, so I vowed to be there for her whenever she wanted to talk. One thing we were both pretty good at!

My head was spinning when I went to bed that night. Now I not only have my cancelled wedding and a charity event to think about, but Mom just lost her job. Over the years I've had the chance to travel with her and see her at work – she is so good at what she does – I can't believe that they would let her go. Again - what a difference a day makes!

It seemed I had just laid my head down when the alarm went off. It was 4:00 a.m. we had to be out of the cottage by 4:30 – we had a 45 minute ride to the airport and a 6:00 a.m. flight to catch. I could hear the shower running so I knew Mom was already up. I could smell coffee, so I knew Dad was up too.

I crawled out of bed and felt like I had a huge load sitting on my shoulders. I wasn't at all sure I was ready to go back to California, but I knew I had to move on. The sooner I got my normal routine in place the better off I'd be. But how could it be normal when so much was different? I would be going to live with my friends Sunni and Mike for awhile until I figured out my next move. I wouldn't be going back to my great little apartment with Kurt. I was no longer engaged. I'm planning a charity event on the opposite coast. And I have to face my co-workers with their looks of sympathy and their words of support.

I also knew I was ready to see Kurt. Not to discuss reconciliation, but to understand what happened and to be able to walk away this time with my head held high.

The ride to the airport was kind of quiet for us. In fact, Mom suggested that I tip my seat back and nap until we arrived. I think we had both said all that there was to say, at least for now.

I hugged Mom good-bye at the airport and promised to call as soon as I landed in San Diego. She promised to keep working on the charity event, but I also made her promise to take some time to think about what she loves, and what she really wants to do with this opportunity that she now has. She agreed, and I was off!

PATTY

It is pitch black out as we are loading up the car to bring Kyle back to the airport. Sherwood is staying at the cottage with Ernie. He is so sad to see Kyle go. I know he will have a little cry when we back out of the driveway. He certainly has a special spot for his little girl.

I'm sad too. I always love being with Kyle, and even though we had a difficult week, it was great having her with us.

She looks so frail to me. I'm sure she has lost more weight, and her eyes have a sadness that I have never seen before. I know she'll be fine, but it will take time. Hopefully having something positive to focus on will help. It should at least make telling her story a little easier.

We hugged good-bye at the curb and I watched her go through the sliding doors to the airport. I'll hear from her again by late afternoon. I hope she can sleep on the plane.

On the drive back to the lake I think about my own day. I want to mail tickets out to my family so they can start giving them away. I will make phone calls to my friends to see if they'd like to attend the charity event. And no doubt I'll have more calls coming in from concerned friends and colleagues regarding my own situation. It will be a busy day!

Sherwood is waiting for me with fresh coffee and donuts when I get back. We sat on the porch and talked. After being assured that Kyle got off fine and would call us later, we began talking about us. What will we do?

The package I will receive from my former company is generous, so there is no immediate cause for concern. I have time to think things through and, as Kyle had mentioned, to focus on what I love.

One thing I love is family, and most of the family is in Vermont. This could be our opportunity to move back home. But then what would I do? I love developing marketing programs and tools, I love managing people, I love planning, and I love training. I could try for a similar position with another life insurance company. Or I could start doing something outside of the financial services industry. I had started reading a book called "Inc. Your Dreams." I think it is time to pull it back out and follow the steps outlined to help guide me through my thought process.

The phone began ringing again. It seemed odd that I was in the position of consoling the people on the other end of the line. I was trying to make them feel better about the fact that I lost my job. Surprisingly, to help me remain positive, I would switch the conversations from my situation to the charity event I was planning with Kyle. One of my favorite female agents out of New York asked to attend and she wanted to bring her daughter with her. I thought that was a beautiful gesture, I was so happy that she would be joining us.

And so the rest of my week went. Phone calls to promote the event, phone calls to accept the condolences of others, and surprisingly, phone calls from several companies already interested in speaking with me about future opportunities.

By the time we headed back to Pennsylvania on Sunday I was talked out!

KYLE

Fortunately my trip home was uneventful. I was able to sleep on both flights!

I arrived at the baggage claim to find my friend Sunni waiting for me. We hugged, and began talking about everything that had happened in the past week, which now seemed like so long ago.

Sunni told me about going to my old apartment and collecting the remainder of my belongings. Of course Kurt was there, and his mother. She said that it was awkward and sad. Kurt looked like hell, which surprisingly didn't make me feel better. In the course of their visit he told them if there was anything I could save from our honeymoon I could have it. I was glad to hear that since I had already invited my mother to join me on the trip to Tahiti, and she accepted my invitation.

When we got back to Sunni's house I unpacked and we sat back with a glass of wine and visited. I was touched to learn that Sunni was planning on coming back East for my charity event. What a great friend! This meant a lot to me.

In the course of our conversation I knew that I wanted to see Kurt one more time. I needed to get closure on everything that had happened. I would call him later in the day.

When I placed the call I could hear the anticipation in his voice, the hope that I may have changed my mind, and the awful sadness of someone that has lost something or someone special. We agreed to meet at a local pub later that afternoon.

I was a bit taken back when I saw Kurt. He looked awful – pale, thin, drawn. He actually looked how I felt.

There was no small talk. We got right to the situation. I really only had one question I needed answered. "Why?"

We talked in circles. More of the same, things I'd already heard. The one question that he was not able to answer for me was the one I was desperate to hear. Kurt could not, or chose not to tell me why.

I hugged him when we parted. He cried, and I just left feeling empty and extremely sad. It was a final good-bye to a life we could have had. My happily ever after – with Kurt Swanson – was completely shattered.

Chapter VIII

PATTY

The remainder of our vacation brought more of the same. Each day I spoke with Kyle to make sure she was doing all right. I hated to hear the sadness in her voice and it left me worrying about her continually. But there was little I could do to help her. I was sure the best I could do for her was to create a successful event, and go with her to Tahiti to continue the healing process.

I spent the next few weeks coordinating the efforts. I was confirming attendance, lining up music, speaking with the charities to make sure they were prepared for their presentations, creating donation tickets, door prize drawings, and organizing a silent auction. The response we were getting from women being invited to the event was so positive. Fortunately many of them were electing to come in on Friday and spend two nights at The Basin Harbor Club. This would definitely help us reduce the room block expense we were now liable for!

While planning the charity event I continued to receive phone calls from caring friends and colleagues regarding the elimination of my position. At night I went to bed so confused over what to do – there were so many opportunities coming my way. A friend of mine, from Atlanta, had suggested that I speak with a friend of hers that is a CEO of a marketing firm in Kansas City. Their company was going through some transition and she felt my planning skills could be of help to them.

I agreed to speak with the CEO, and the result of our conversation was he invited me to Kansas to meet with him and his company. Our first meeting was over dinner. We got along great – but both of us were working on different agendas. I went to the meeting having made the decision to start my own consulting firm, which would allow me to live wherever I wanted and do what I loved. He went to the meeting wanting to hire me as a recruiter – a fulltime position within his company. We both seemed surprised at the end of the night when he made his offer and I declined! It was agreed that I'd come into the company the next day to get a better feel for what they do. He obviously was proud and excited over what he had built, and I was anxious to see his operation.

He was a perfect host. He introduced me to all of his management team, and then had me meet with one of his female recruiters. Her job was to convince me that this would be a great job. As we were meeting I let her know that I really wasn't interested. Instead, I started asking her questions regarding the firm's marketing. We had a great meeting. She was excited over the marketing idea I shared and wanted to make sure that I shared these with the CEO.

As I joined him in his office, he was meeting with his CFO. He said, "Now that you have seen the company – what do you think?" I responded with, "I think that you need a consultant!"

Both men laughed at that and I began discussing my observations and sharing my ideas. I could see the excitement building in him as we talked. He called in his assistant to ask to have a lunch arranged with several of his marketing team.

Lunch was a great exchange of ideas. As we were walking out of the restaurant the two gentlemen that had joined us asked, "How soon can we get you working with us?" My response was that it was up to Rod, the CEO. Up until this point he hadn't wanted to hire a consultant!

When we returned to the office, behind Rod's closed door, the negotiations began. I left having been hired "exclusively, for a flat monthly fee." We had also scheduled a follow-up visit the next week where I would work with his management team to develop a priority list of projects.

I was on cloud nine when I left. My first meeting as a consultant and I had landed an exclusive contract that paid as much as I was making for base salary in my previous position.

At the airport waiting for my flight I called my husband and two of my best friends. In retrospect I probably sounded like an idiot – but I was very excited!!! Everything had fallen into place. I was a consultant!

I took the assignment very seriously and on the flight home began writing their first brochure. I was very anxious to go back and get really focused on meeting their needs.

The next week I returned to Kansas and spent a few days with the firm. I sat in product meetings, participated in two top producer meetings, joined a management meeting to talk about product road shows, and developed a priority list of projects. The list was three pages long – there were so many opportunities here. I was in heaven – I would be developing marketing programs and tools to help position them for recruiting and sales.

In my brief time there I felt that I had already demonstrated the value I could bring to the organization.

When I returned home I had a limited amount of time to devote to the consulting job as I would soon be leaving for Vermont. But with the little time I had, I jumped in feet first and began working on the priority list.

In the midst of this Sherwood and I decided to sell the Pennsylvania house and move back to Vermont. It was the perfect opportunity. Sherwood couldn't have been happier with our decision. We put the house on the market immediately. We listed with our former neighbor and friend. An open house would be planned for the next week when we were in Vermont.

I spent the last week in Pennsylvania burning the midnight oil. I was anxious to make a dent on the marketing materials we had identified. As I completed them I sent them on to the CEO. I also was crossing my t's and dotting my i's for the charity event which was just around the corner.

One of the charities we had chosen, CARE, had a media person that had asked permission to promote Kyle's story. Kyle had agreed to help build support for the charities, but what she really wanted was to focus on the charity – not on the broken engagement. And she would not share the name of her former fiancée.

In the meantime, a friend of mine from Vermont had called a local Vermont paper and told them about Kyle's story. With Kyle's permission, the day before I left for Vermont I was interviewed by a reporter from the *Barre-Montpelier Times Argus*. They wanted to do a story on Kyle, a local girl that had a taken a bad experience and turned it into something positive.

In talking to Kyle I learned that CARE had also spoken to her about some media opportunities. Although a bit reluctant, Kyle agreed to support their efforts.

Certainly the event, and now some media, would help take Kyle's mind off of her personal heartache. I was praying for that. I couldn't wait to see her again, which was now just a few days away. I would arrive in Vermont on Sunday and she would join us on Monday.

KYLE

The next month was a bit of a blur to me. I moved in with my girlfriend Lisa who had a two bedroom house not far from where I had lived. Luckily we got along great and for now it was good to be with a friend. With the price of apartments in the San Diego area I wasn't prepared to spend what it would take to restart on my own.

I went through the motions of work. It seemed that daily I had to relay my story to someone new. I was tiring of the sympathetic looks and all the questions. But I also spoke to my family daily and my friends remained a constant for me, always there to lend their support.

I was in contact on a regular basis with our charities as well. CARE had called and asked if I would be willing to share my story. I felt like that was all I'd been doing, but if it would help them I would. I did set a few guidelines. I wanted to focus on the charity aspect, I did not want to talk about the details of my broken engagement, and I would not mention the name of my former fiancé. As angry as I had been, I knew that wouldn't be fair to him or his family.

At work everyone was so supportive, even members of the Club. It was amazing the impact my story was having on those around me. LaCosta donated lodging from two of their properties for our silent auction, people were writing checks for the charities, and friends from around the country were planning to go to Vermont to show their support. Not just women that would be attending the event, but many of my guy friends were coming too. I don't know if they realized how important that was to me.

CARE called to let me know that the New York Times wanted to write a story. A reporter came by and interviewed me. They took a picture and said that they would publish the article the day of the event.

The process was painless, the reporter was easy to talk to and I was confident that the focus would be positioned as I had requested.

My mother and I were going back and forth with speeches, making tweaks, and preparing to tell the story from each of our perspectives.

I went shopping for a new dress. My beautiful wedding gown had been delivered to my parent's house, only to be buried in their closet for God only knows how long – maybe I'd wear it one day, or maybe I'd sell it on eBay. But now I needed something beautiful to wear. I found a perfect white strapless dress, simple and elegant. I had lost so much weight that I had to get a size smaller than normal...this was a bit concerning to me...I wasn't sure that I liked being a size 0.

Then I received another call from CARE. A women's radio show wanted me to be their guest, to share my story. I agreed and was interviewed on live radio. I have to say they made it fun, and the hostess made me feel so good about what I was doing. They were completely behind my theme of Women Make a Difference. When our call ended they asked me to come back on again after the event and let them know how it went. I agreed.

On September 4th I flew back to Vermont for the beginning of what would be yet another life altering week.

PATTY

Sherwood and I were back at the cottage for Labor Day weekend. I'd been making final plans for the charity event and anxiously waiting for Kyle to come join us. I cannot wait to see her. This is going to be another tough week for her. I have been so impressed with her strength and her spirit. She has been coping well with an awful situation.

As I watched her get off the plane I was taken aback by her weight loss, she looked so thin and frail. But she also looked beautiful and confident. I was so proud of her.

We hugged and began talking a mile a minute, each of us trying to bring the other up to date on everything that was happening in our lives – from the event to the "honeymoon" to my new business. I have to say, I think we were both counting down to get the event behind us – we were very excited to take our trip! She would leave on Monday, and we would meet in LA on Tuesday. But from now until then there was still a lot to do! Plus we wanted to enjoy the last of the beautiful weather on the lake.

Chapter IX

PATTY

The week flew by for us. Working side by side we put the finishing touches on our signage for the silent auction, we worked on seating charts, and we practiced our speeches.

The program was going to involve a lot of family. Everyone wanted to take on a role. People were excited for the event. We were excited too, but also a bit apprehensive. I was so worried that this was going to be too hard for Kyle. Would she be able to withstand the pressure? Would she be able to attend an event that should have been her wedding to support charities instead? Time would tell.

Many of our guests were going to be arriving on Friday so we were still going to have a dinner that evening for friends and family traveling in. Those on "our side" that had booked rooms for the wedding kept their reservations, thankfully, and decided to make a weekend of it.

Friday morning we were on our way. Sherwood was going to come over in the morning to wish Kyle well.

Our first order of the day was to visit the Vermont Children's Aid Society to meet the Executive Director and his team face-to-face. It would be our first meeting with them. We had no sooner driven away from the cottage, however, when my cell phone rang. It was Sherwood. He had just gotten a phone call from Channel 3 News in Burlington,

VT – from the local news anchor himself, Marcellus Parsons. He wanted to interview Kyle for the evening news. Evidently her story had just been published in the Times Argus.

We stopped for a paper and, much to our surprise; it was the front page story. "The wedding's off, but not the party" Former Barre Town girl makes best of it after fiancés affront, by David Delcore.

KYLE

What is going on? My story is on the front page of the paper, and now they want me to do a TV interview? This is a bit more than I was prepared for. Little did I know it would soon get worse.

I called Channel 3, which is the local CBS affiliate, and we arranged for the interview. They wanted to talk to Mom and Me at The Basin Harbor Club. They would meet us there in the afternoon. Their plan was to put a spot on the 6:00 p.m. news.

I decided I'd worry about that later. For now I was going to call Vermont Children's Aid Society and let them know we were on our way. When Steve picked up the phone, he sounded panic stricken. Now what was wrong? I soon learned.

Evidently the New York Times article had been published a day earlier than we expected and the national news media had picked up on it. In Winooski, Vermont, a little charity that had never been able to get any publicity was sitting there with the TV show Inside Edition in their office. They wanted to interview Kyle…what was he suppose to do? Clearly panic had set in.

When I got off the phone I looked at my mother and just said, "What do you think I've gotten myself into?" I relayed the conversation to her, and we didn't know whether to laugh or cry. Suddenly a lot was happening around us that was turning our event into something we had never expected. We stopped for a copy of The New York Times and I was a bit taken back by the title, "Wedding Off, Jilted Bride Turns Party into a Benefit." There was the article and my picture with a caption below that read, Kyle Paxman won't be saying "I do" as planned, but heartbreak or not, the reception will go on, with a new focus: philanthropy.

Although I didn't like the title of the article I loved the concept of the story, and for the first time it hit me that I was being philanthropic. It felt good. It actually felt really good. I may never have another opportunity like this in my lifetime to give to others and make an impact. It was a heavy thought. A thought that for the first time made me realize that I had really been given a gift through all my heartache – wow! It was quite a revelation!

We arrived at Vermont Children's Aid Society and were greeted by Steve, and we met the camera man and reporter from Inside Edition. While they set-up their equipment we went to Steve's office to review the evening ahead. He had three women from the organization that would speak Saturday evening, and he was going to attend "in the background" to take pictures and see the event unfold.

A reporter from The Burlington Free Press had also just arrived and was hoping to speak with us for a few minutes. Mariana Lamaison Sears interviewed us. I liked her, and invited her to attend the event as a guest. She said she'd be there.

We were all getting a little nervous by this time. They were ready to film. Mom gave me a hug and the door was closed behind me. For the next half hour we visited. It wasn't nearly as stressful as I had anticipated. I just answered their questions – clearly they were on my side – and I told them all they wanted to know about the event we had planned. With our permission, they also wanted to take some photos at the Basin Harbor Club.

From Winooski we drove to Vergennes. The plan was to check-in, walk through the event, and begin greeting our guests who would soon be arriving.

When we checked in we were shocked to have email messages waiting for us. One from an old high school friend of my mothers, some from my friends, and others from people we had never heard of. It was amazing to us that my little story was generating such outreach, caring, and support.

I had little time to reflect on what was happening as CBS was there to do my interview.

PATTY

I can't begin to describe how proud I was of Kyle.

We met the reporter and the camera man. They wanted to see where the ceremony would have taken place. Then I sat back and watched them film, and felt my heart break!

Walking down the marble path from the "bridal suite" to the place the ceremony would have taken place was my beautiful daughter. But she wasn't dressed as the beautiful bride on the arm of her father. Rather, she was a beautiful, confident, woman walking with a reporter and answering his questions. I could have lain down on the lawn and sobbed. This was not the way it was suppose to be. She deserved so much more. She had planned so much more.

In those moments it was apparent I had raised her to be a brave, strong, proud woman. She showed so much maturity and poise. I couldn't have loved her more!

They then wanted to ask me a few questions. I think I would have been fine if the first question hadn't been "What are you thinking when you look at your daughter right now?" All my emotions came to surface. I think I told them that I couldn't be more proud of her…but then again, my emotions were so raw I could barely speak!

We spent a few more minutes with them as they filmed the two of us walking across the grounds together.

When the CBS crew left, Kyle and I went our separate ways. She went to greet some of her friends and I went to meet with the wedding coordinator and the CFO of The Basin Harbor Club. I must say they were amazing. I went through the details of the charity event with them, and made arrangements to meet with them again on Sunday morning to "settle up." They didn't want me to worry about it now.

So I too went to greet family and friends. We would all be getting together at "the Red Barn" for dinner in a few hours.

KYLE

I was pleased when the interview with CBS was over. I think it went well. Understanding of the philanthropic opportunity in front of me had helped make all the difference. The sorrow of not getting married was there, but not at the forefront.

The reporter was wonderful. He made me feel like I was talking to my Dad – Sherwood. He was comforting and concerned. He was kind and caring. At the moment I felt worse for my mother than for me. She clearly looked upset…but she was watching me with her encouraging smile.

As we had planned the wedding I sometimes thought that it was as much for Mom as for me. She'd never had the big wedding. She was trying to give me everything she had never had, memories that would last a lifetime. In retrospect, I think the charity event helped her take her mind of the loss of not seeing all our plans come to fruition. Her sadness in not seeing her daughter married to the man of her dreams. But – we moved on.

Then I saw my friends! Some came from California, some from St. John. All were special people in my life. It was great to see them… Adam, Toby, Chris, and their girlfriends, all of whom would be at the event.

My brother and his family arrived next, followed by my aunts, and their guests. It really began feeling light hearted and festive!

When we went to our room to get ready for dinner a bottle of Dom Perignon had been delivered from a stranger, someone touched by my story! Messages were lighting up our phone from around the world – people wishing me luck with my charity event. It was like nothing I'd ever experienced in my life.

PATTY

In the midst of all the preparations, the people from CARE arrived, and we spent some time getting to know them. But we had a schedule to keep!

Kyle and I got ready for dinner and went to join our guests. We all had cocktails together while waiting to see Kyle's news spot. When it came on, the whole restaurant cheered and watched in awe. She was amazing! She looked gorgeous and really did a great job. I have to admit that I didn't look half bad myself.

We moved into the banquet room and enjoyed a great dinner with family and friends. Over the course of the night several hotel guests that were not part of our group brought us donations. They had been touched by Kyle too. It really was humbling.

We thought we had experienced the end of the media blitz, until the next morning arrived.

KYLE

We woke to a phone call from CARE's PR person. Evidently my story had generated a lot of buzz. People were calling from around the World. The Today Show, Good Morning America, Dr. Phil, The Ellen Show, The View, Dr. Keith, The London Times, The German Times, Glamour Magazine, and more. They all wanted to have me on their shows. Some wanted to come and film my event. This had quickly jumped way out of proportion.

Mom, my cousin Misty and I went to breakfast, which helped us relax – at least for awhile. Then we realized that reporters had started arriving, all wanting to interview me and Mom.

I had a few minutes of feeling completely overwhelmed. Our guests were so excited, just to be a part of all this. I started to get mad at my mother because I thought she was forgetting what this day was supposed to have been – my wedding. She was "in the moment". One of my friends took me out for a walk by the lake, and then some of our friends joined me. This was what I needed. It gave me a minute to reflect, relax, and regroup.

In the meantime my mother came back to earth and took charge of keeping people away from me, including reporters. We were being stalked by a reporter from The Boston Globe, who wouldn't leave. Mom finally did the interview with him to allow me more time with friends.

PATTY

When I awoke my first thoughts went to Kyle. I said a prayer that she would continue to be brave, strong and proud as she went through the day – her wedding day. We spoke about it, and she seemed sad but ready for what lied ahead of us. Little did we know, however, exactly what that was going to be.

As we went into the dining room for breakfast I could not believe the excitement that seemed to be in the air. Everyone was so excited about the media blitz taking place before our eyes.

People had newspapers spread out on the tables, Kyle was the feature of AOL, calls were shutting down the phone system at The Basin Harbor Club, and their web-site was getting more hits than they'd ever received. I felt myself fall into the excitement with the others. Until I got "the look" from Kyle – it is one I have had the pleasure of seeing only occasionally over the years – she was ticked off at me.

This time however, it hit me like a brick. How insensitive was I being? My daughter should be getting ready for her walk down the aisle today – instead she's going to host a charity event – and I'm excited. We are all excited! It knocked me down to earth in a hurry. I was so sorry; all I could do now was whatever it would take to give her the space she needed. Knowing Kyle, the best thing for her would be time with her friends.

I asked the front desk to take messages and not allow calls through to our room. I asked CARE to manage the other calls coming in. Then I spoke to the reporter from The Boston Globe. The reporter was Michael Levenson. He was a great young man and truly seemed to be personally touched by Kyle. When I asked him why he thought she was getting all this attention he told me that although many people have had to cancel weddings, few had taken the experience and turned it into something so positive to help others.

When I returned to the room Sherwood had arrived to give his support to Kyle and wish her well. She asked him to stay but he didn't want to get in the way of her day.

While he was still with us we spoke to the PR person from CARE again. They were organizing the media. Due to the overwhelming interest in the story we decided to open the event up to a limited group and we would be interviewed. At 4:00 the selected group would meet us in one of the party rooms.

We were going to have a press conference.

Chapter X

KYLE

Of the four women I had chosen to be in my wedding, only one came to Vermont for the event. Sunni arrived shortly after we had learned that we would be having a press conference. She was a God send!

Sunni is amazingly calming. She also is an artist with make-up! As soon as she arrived she joined Mom and me and did our make-up. I honestly had gone a little pale through all of this, so I was ready for some magic!

We got dressed in our outfits for the evening. I wore my beautiful new short white dress with a baby blue shawl from Sunni. Mom wore the outfit she had bought for the wedding. She looked so nice in a beautiful pink chiffon skirt and jacket. We were ready. My brother, Keith, had come to give me his support.

We rode from our cottage to the Press Conference – it was a short ride, but it seemed long at the time. I'll never forget Keith holding my hand and walking me up the stairs. I felt safe with him by my side, once again, the protected little sister.

When we got in the building they ushered us into a kitchen area and told us what to expect. There were five groups present – The Today

Show, Good Morning America, Inside Edition, The Boston Globe and The Burlington Free Press. We would be interviewed for five minutes only. The PR person from CARE would manage the time. Cameras would be rolling as soon as we opened the door.

It was time. We were brought in and sat in two chairs in front of a swarm of reporters and cameras.

PATTY

I spent the afternoon rushing to get the event in order. I made sure the room was set perfectly, the silent auction items were well presented, and everyone helping us knew their jobs. There wasn't much more I could do but wait.

As I headed to our cottage it began raining, a final sign that the wedding wasn't meant to be. Fortunately, we had moved the reception inside earlier as a precaution.

When I got back to the room I found out about the Press Conference and was glad that Sunni had come to help us get ready. I had wanted to take a hot shower, redo my hair, and relax, but there was now no time. We were on the move.

The people from CARE were there taking pictures of us getting ready, interviewing us for their own PR. But here was Kyle – amazing again. Taking everything in stride, she was calm! We had guests in our living room having cocktails and visiting. Keith and Julia were in the cottage next door – he was going to go with us to the Press Conference. I was so proud of him. He was really there for Kyle, giving her so much love and support. What a great son, what a great brother!

Sunni finished Kyle's make-up and she looked lovely. It was my turn. I'd never had my make-up done by someone else before and I really wasn't too sure I wanted to now. But, Kyle wanted me to – so I sat back and tried to relax.

I was actually pleased with the results. It was subtle, however my hair – that wasn't doing it for me. But, we were out of time.

During our short ride to the press conference I kept thinking how "out of control" this charity event had become. Normally I would have been at the reception making sure all the finishing touches were in place. I would have been greeting our guests as they arrived. Instead, I was going to participate in a press conference – with bad hair!

KYLE

The questions started immediately.
Tell us how you learned about your fiancée?
How did you feel?
What did you do?
When did you decide to turn your wedding into a charity event?
How did you select your charities?
Why focus on women? Why no men? Are you anti-men now?
What could I do now but take a deep breath and answer their questions? I spoke from my heart and hoped that I made some sense. I held my mother's hand – it calmed us both. My brother was watching from the sidelines – snapping his own pictures. This made me want to laugh out loud. He was going to get his own story – I loved it – I loved him!

PATTY

I have loved Kyle forever, and have always been proud of her. But at this time, at this moment, I couldn't have felt more love or more pride for her. She was eloquent with her answers. She was calm. She was perfect. Thankfully, most of the questions were directed at her, as I was holding my breath waiting to see what would come my way.

My questions were:

What did you hope to gain by convincing Kyle to hold a charity event?

What do you think of her now?

How would you describe your daughter?

Easy questions. I had hoped to give Kyle something positive to focus on to make the pain of not getting married easier for her.

We had both agreed that healing began when we focused our attention on helping others.

What do you think of her now – the same as always – she was an amazing woman, I love her more than words can describe, and I was proud of her. I remember describing her as a beautiful woman outside and in. I think that summed it up!

The Press Conference ended and we briefly went back to our cottage to catch our breath. Before we knew it, it was time to be at the reception. We entered the room ready to meet our guests. The cameras were rolling there as well. Not only was our every move being filmed, but our guests were being interviewed by reporters as well.

Family, friends, and strangers were hugging us. They were congratulating Kyle on her bravery. We laughed, we cried, and then we moved on to the dinner and main event.

KYLE

As we walked through the door, I couldn't help but think what a beautiful cocktail reception this would have been for a wedding. The room was beautiful and the appetizers looked wonderful.

There were cheese plates, fruit plates, and dips in the center island. Hot and cold apps were being passed around by the white gloved attendants. It was very elegant.

But there was no time to dwell on that – people were waiting to speak with Mom and me. Cameras were snapping, the press was interviewing everyone. I was so happy to see all the women that had turned out for my event. My Nana who hates too much "hoopla" was there (looking incredibly sweet); Julia, my sister-in-law was there with my niece McKenna – our youngest family member at seven months old; Rose, Sherri, Nicole, Danielle, Aunt Kathy, Aunt Jeanne, Aunt Barbara, Aunt Laurie, Aunt Diane, Aunt Michelle, and so many friends – all were there. I felt truly blessed.

I watched my mother make her way through the crowd. She was the perfect hostess. I felt her strength and it helped carry me. She was feeling mine as well. We would speak later about how we helped each other through the night. Together we were strong. There was and always will be a special bond between us.

After a few moments, I was amazed to find how it was easy to forget about the cameras. This was a room full of beautiful strong woman, women that cared about me. The cause was great. It was going to be an emotional, but wonderful night.

Chapter XI

PATTY

Kyle and I waited for the guests to be escorted across the driveway to the Green Mountain Room where the dinner was being held. Then together we walked over to join them.

Women were already viewing the silent auction items, drinks were being served, the band had set-up, and people were finding their tables. We would be at the head table right in front of the podium.

Within a few minutes people were asked to take their seats and the program began.

Julia, my daughter-in-law, was emcee for the first half of the program. She looked adorable in a white and green floral print dress. She appeared very comfortable as she took her position at the microphone.

She introduced herself and thanked everyone for coming. When she acknowledged the distance some people traveled it was truly amazing. We had guests from St. John, California, Washington, Florida, New Hampshire, Maine, New York, New Jersey, Pennsylvania, Georgia, and of course from all over the state of Vermont. As she mentioned the states we knew about, people were shouting out other states. The support was amazing.

I was the first speaker. I felt good. I was no stranger to public speaking, so I was prepared. What I wasn't prepared for was the emotion I would feel when I looked into the audience and saw the love and concern coming from everyone out there, and then of course there was Kyle. Again, I was taken aback by the look of pure strength in her.

I began my speech. My job was to share our story, from our perspective, with everyone. So in our words our guests heard of the events that lead us to this moment. From Kyle getting the news, to joining me in Vermont, to planning a charity event, our guests were glued to the story. My voice quivered as I talked about it, as I shared Kyle's painful story and all that had transpired between then and now. I ended my talk by introducing everyone to my daughter. I told her how much I loved her and how proud I was of her.

Then it was her turn! My strong, beautiful daughter was about to speak and demonstrate to this crowd of 125 women how amazing she really is. They would soon see what I have always known: she is beautiful from the outside in.

KYLE

I was so pleased with Julia's opening comments. They were light, they included everyone in the room, and they were spoken right from her heart. She introduced Mom and they hugged. Mom took the podium.

It's funny that it reminded me at first of being a little girl. My mother belonged to Toastmasters and would practice her speeches in front of me. I always loved listening to them and she would let me critique her when she was done. Even though I was just a kid she listened to what I had to say like she really cared, and she would often make the changes I suggested. I always thought that was pretty cool of her. She would also have me count how many "ums" and "ahs", and for every one I caught she'd pay me a quarter. I never got too rich on it, but it taught me the importance of practice. Ever since then when I hear someone speak it is the one thing I always pick up on. It is also the one mistake neither of us make.

Mom captured the room as soon as she spoke. She relayed our story from a mother's perspective. I could hear the occasional quiver in her voice and realized how emotional it would be for her to share so much detail with a room full of people. But she was strong too. Her message demonstrated the strength we all have within us and focused on staying positive -- even in the midst of adversity. It was obvious how much she loved me, and how much having me hurt, hurt her as well. As I looked around the room it was clear, there wasn't a dry eye in the house.

As Mom introduced me I joined her up front, we gave each other a hug and I could feel her strength flow through me. I was ready for the task ahead.

My story was a bit different. It really was a tribute to my mother. I spoke of the lessons learned from childhood. I spoke of the words she used with me so often in letters, in phone conversations, and on the day I shared with her my news – be brave, be strong, and be proud. I spoke of the power that was within those words, and the impact they had made in my life. I also shared some news that wasn't common knowledge – that wasn't part of any headline news story. It was the story of my mother losing her job just days after we cancelled a wedding and planned this event. The point of sharing this was not to have anyone feel sorry for her, but to understand that she practiced what she preached – the importance of words and actions. She always looked for the positive and showed the power we have within ourselves to create our experiences.

The story of my mother lead me to the charities we had chosen. I spoke of the great opportunity this tragedy had given to me, the opportunity to help others, the opportunity to make a difference, and the opportunity to be philanthropic – never before had I been given so much. Amazingly, that is truly how I felt. I was happy that I had learned the truth about my fiancé, and I was grateful to the man that shared the story with me. I was thankful that I had such supportive family and friends, I was grateful that my parents stood behind my decisions without hesitation, and I was grateful that we had chosen to do a charity event in place of a wedding. I was also thankful that we had found two wonderful charities to promote.

That is not to say I wasn't in pain. My heart was still hurting and broken. I would have loved to have been having all of our guests there to celebrate my marriage, and sharing in my happiness rather than my sorrow.

I ended my speech with a few thank yous of my own and a toast.

I said, "So to Mom – I love you so much. Thank you from the bottom of my heart for being you. For being there for me and for having taught me, by example, how to be brave, be strong and be proud.

To each of you – thank you for believing in this cause, thank you for being here, and thank you for supporting me and these two special charities.

Please raise your glasses and let's toast…
Here's to the women of the world!"

The room stood in applause as I finished. Many were openly sobbing as I sat back down. Our story had touched their hearts.

Julia had to stand back up and end this portion of the program, which she did. She also proposed a toast, this one for me. She thanked me for being her sister-in-law and friend, and she thanked me for being a role model for her daughter McKenna. When she was through we hugged, and we cried, and everyone joined us…

Dinner was served!

PATTY

Kyle's speech was touching and much of it was a tribute to me. I wanted to put my head on the table and sob — but of course I didn't. Instead I looked at her and we held eye contact through much of her speech. I could tell she was giving it for me. My heart was full.

She ended her speech with class, as she toasted the women of the world. I was so proud of her.

Then Julia paid tribute to Kyle with heartfelt toast of her own.

With not a dry eye in the house I wasn't sure how anyone was going to be able to eat a bite. Actually I don't think Kyle or I did. Rather than eat, we spent most of the meal going from table to table thanking people for being there. We let each of them know how much having them there meant to us.

As we mingled with guests, my sister Jeanne announced that it was their final opportunity to bid on silent auction items, and my sister Kathy paid tribute to women of strength that had passed before us. Kyle and I had looked at the guest lists and pulled the names of women who we knew had had an impact on someone else in the audience during their life. We recognized grandmothers, mothers, daughters, aunts, and close friends. It was a little gesture that helped everyone personally connect to our theme of "women make a difference."

Dessert was then served. You should have seen the cake — it was beautiful. It was the actual wedding cake – four squared layers on pillars with fresh flowers. But rather than the crystal S that was planned for the top there were flowers and a note which read: "Women Make a Difference." It was a chocolate cake with butter cream frosting – Kyle's favorite.

A funny thing, we saved the top, and one year later Kyle and I had a piece. It was still delicious…in fact, we enjoyed it more the second time!

KYLE

The meals looked wonderful, the presentation was great, but I had no appetite, which was nothing new to me lately. So rather than eat I went visiting from one table to the next. I thanked each person there for taking the time and caring enough to be with us. I laughed when I noticed my mother doing the exact same thing – she started on the opposite side of the room.

I was thankful that my aunts were keeping things moving for us. The silent auction ended, tributes had been paid to women who went before us, and now door prizes were being drawn. We had everyone register when they arrived. Our gifts were candles and jewelry boxes honoring Susan B. Kohan's fight for breast cancer. The winners loved them, all in pale pink.

Another gesture we had made was to give everyone a silver engraved picture frame. They would have been used at my wedding. We had engraved the date – September 9, 2006. Rather than a picture there now was a note "Women make a difference."

I opted not to cut the cake, which would have been a beautiful wedding cake! Each piece was served with a chocolate covered strawberry. Yum.

My step-sister Sherri was the emcee for the second half of the program which began as dessert was being served. This was each charity's opportunity to say a few words about their mission. We wanted people to understand who they were, who they served, and the value they bring.

We began with the Vermont Children's Aid Society. They had three women present, each of whom spoke briefly about their programs: adoption, kids-a-part (for children of incarcerated parents), and counseling. Their stories were touching and hearing the difference that just a few dollars could make to their programs was motivating.

CARE followed, and they too had three women present. One was the person who received my initial phone call; another shared the programs they support; and the third was the public relations person that had helped spread the word of our story – but more importantly, who had just helped us survive our press conference. When she finished her speech she asked me to join them up front. They presented me with a beautiful framed picture of women. Women that had been in the commercial we had initially seen that helped us select CARE as one of our charities. It was beautiful, and still proudly hangs in my bedroom today.

The program ended with my Aunt Barbara. Her job was to ask everyone present to donate to one of our two charities in honor of me. Again we needed tissues! Her talk was so emotional as she addressed the value of strength in women and the difference giving can make. She certainly ended with a call to action. Everyone was picking up their donation cards and filling them out!

Sherri wrapped the program up with another thank you, and people began to mingle.

It was such a relief – the hard part was over. The program had been amazing. Those that were in attendance loved it. The charities had made an impact – but so had my family. I really was blessed to have such strong women in my life...my Mom, my Aunts, my Nana who was responsible for all of them, my cousin, my sisters, my sister-in-law, and my beautiful niece McKenna! Looking at all of them I knew I would be ok too.

The music played, women danced together, cocktails were served, and we all talked. People were telling us things like, "tonight just made me want to go home and hug my daughter", "I am going to get closer to my mother again," "I wish my sister was here with me." And, there were more – everyone had something wonderful to say.

And that's when I realized – the cameras had been rolling all night long. We were so caught in the moment that we really lost sight of that. That was a surprising revelation. Since initially we were afraid they'd distract from the night, what a surprise it was to discover that once we got going nobody cared! Still, I was happy to realize they had left.

PATTY

I can breathe again. Everything went off without a hitch. It was beautiful. I'm so happy to see Kyle catching up with her friends. She's laughing, and she appears to actually be having fun.

The two charities are in another room tallying up the donations. I've checked in on them, they seem to be happy. Before people leave I know that Kyle wants to announce how much we were able to bring in for our charities.

We quietly slipped in to find out our total. We were hoping for at least $12,500 – which would have been equal to an average of $100 per person. We were floored when we heard we were at almost $19,000! It was almost split evenly between the two charities. So, I made a decision to make them even and bring our grand total to $20,000 – with both getting exactly $10,000. I figured at this point what's another $1,000!

Kyle was beside herself with excitement. She ran to the podium to announce the good news. In one night our room full of women truly made a difference. We were able to raise $20,000. The room cheered!

People that had driven in for the event then started to leave. Those of us who were staying over decided to go and celebrate a great event. We all went to The Red Barn and danced until they shut the doors. Women, dancing with women, filled the dance floor – all were celebrating a great night!

I have to admit I was exhausted, and my feet were killing me. But it felt good and I was happy for Kyle, that she was able to stay so positive and so strong all night long.

We went back to our room, but Kyle, Misty and Barbara weren't ready to call it a night. Not yet.

KYLE

I was so proud to tell everyone how much we had collected for our two charities. I have never in my life been in a position to donate much to charity. To realize that because of me – and I don't mean "just me" but everyone who pulled together to make "my event" a success – we were able to raise $20,000 in one evening was overwhelming.

When it was time to leave the "event" and go celebrate our success I was more than ready. We danced, we laughed, and we drank.

We met a lot of people there who knew of my story, and all were congratulating me! Then I was approached by a young couple that wanted to thank me. I wasn't sure why they'd be thanking me until they shared their story. They were young, they both worked at the Basin Harbor Club, and they didn't have much money between them. They had hoped that they'd be able to get married in the gardens on property. Because of my wedding they couldn't. However, when the wedding canceled and we moved our activities inside, the opportunity opened up for them. So in between rain drops they got married on my day, in my spot. They were so happy. I was so happy for them. Another unplanned gift!

As we continued to talk we found out that they had been given one of the cottages from the resort for a wedding gift – one of the ones that we had originally had guests booked in. It was a good turn of events for them.

When we returned to the room, I was still restless. So with a little convincing, Aunt Barbara, Misty and I took my bottle of Dom Perignon and went to join the party of the newlyweds a few doors down.

It was a great ending to our night!

Just as we were leaving someone from the resort was showing up to break up the party. Apparently another cottage had complained of all the noise. Since it was after 4:00 a.m. they felt it was time to call it a night.

As it turned out it was my brother in the cottage next door. Little did he know that I was in the middle of the party he just had closed down!

Charity Event – Women Make a Difference

Chapter XII

KYLE

I woke to the phone ringing. Luckily mom answered it, but she was soon in my room to see if we were awake yet. Evidently what we thought had just ended was somehow just beginning.

The Basin Harbor Club had been inundated with phone calls over the weekend, and with today's newspapers the calls increased.

The Boston Sunday Globe published their article. The Burlington Free Press had published a touching story about me on the first page of the Neighbors section. The Today Show called and wanted to do an expanded story – including another interview, pictures from our honeymoon and a live appearance. Add to that hundreds of emails from people we didn't know.

Now that it was over, I wanted it to be over. I would have to make a decision on just how much publicly I would be willing to do for the sake of charity. Every meeting would be like opening my heartache up again.

But, now wasn't the time to make that decision – I needed coffee!!!

We got ready and went to breakfast to say good bye to our guests.

PATTY

I heard Kyle and Misty come in really late last night, or really early this morning! I'm sure she is not going to want to deal with all of these decisions that now need to be made. Hopefully they can wait.

When we got to breakfast we met family and friends again – they all had newspapers in front of them. Kyle's story seemed to be everywhere. They were all wonderfully written.

To everyone else the prospect of being on TV was very exciting. They all had a favorite show that they thought she should appear on. Since the requests now were extensive – Dr. Phil – my niece Anna loved him, my mother loved The View, I loved Ellen and I liked that she had asked Kyle to be on her show as one of her first "ordinary people that do extraordinary things." There were so many requests that the big joke was where's Oprah, since that is the one show that Kyle actually would have liked to go on.

I was proud of how she was handling all of this. With a grain of salt, and a lot of maturity, she didn't seem to be as wrapped up in the media sensation as everyone else was.

I still had one more important meeting. I was meeting with the wedding coordinator from the Basin Harbor Club and their CFO. It was time to write the final check. I knew what the wedding cost was going to be – so I was ready for that. But today we would also find out exactly how much more I had to pay in unused rooms. It could push close to $45,000. Thankfully, some of the rooms were filled and "the groom's family" had offered to pay for the ones they had booked. So I went to my meeting prepared to write another good sized check.

There was something about the CFO that, every time he spoke to me, I felt like sobbing. I think because he was a father of little girls himself that he had a different level of compassion – a kindness that just seemed to come out of his eyes when he spoke. He had a wonderful way about him, which was kind of unusual based on the CFOs I've known from the past. The first thing he did was congratulate me on our event. Then he went on to share with me the impact Kyle's story had had on the resort.

The Basin Harbor Club's website had more activity in the last two days than it had had since it was launched. Three people had booked weddings, and their phone was ringing off the hook. Because of this, and because he felt it was "the right thing to do" they were not going to charge me for any of the unused/unpaid rooms. I could have sobbed – oh yeah, wait a minute -- I did sob!

KYLE

As we said good bye to our last guests it was time to pack up and join Dad back at the cottage in Alburgh and relax for the rest of the day. I was ready for that.

Mom and I spent the hour long ride talking about all that had happened. Jon called, (he had checked in on me throughout the week), wanting to know how the event went. He was shocked at what we were able to raise, and more shocked over the media attention we had received. We told him that in the eyes of 125 women at our event he was a hero. He laughed at that.

Dad was there to greet us when we drove in to the yard. He was so proud of us both. Typical of Dad he had a nice lunch all ready for us to enjoy.

Now that the event was behind us we started talking about the honeymoon! I would be leaving for home in the morning, and I would meet Mom in LA on Tuesday. We were both looking forward to 10 days of sand and sunshine.

We talked about the media requests and I made a decision. I would do only two shows. I would do the Today show, and I would do the Ellen Show, and that was it. I didn't want to continue being known as "the Jilted Bride". I wanted to move on now and try to get this all be behind me. It seemed like a good plan!

In the morning I said good-bye to Dad, before Mom took me to the airport. He hugged me and told me again how proud he was of me. The night before he made it clear that if I found it too difficult in California now, there would always be a place for me with him and Mom until I decided what I wanted to do and where I wanted to be. Since the day I left college I hadn't lived with my parents, and as much as I loved them both, I was sure I didn't want to live with them now.

His final words were to make sure that Mom and I had a great trip – we both deserved it!

I said bye to Mom at the airport. Our hugs were happy hugs this time. We made it through the week, and we were excited about the trip we'd be taking. We would see each other tomorrow in LA.

When I landed – Jon was there to pick me up.

PATTY

I was so pleased with the way everything had turned out. We made it through what would have been Kyle's wedding day, and she survived. We all survived. It was time to move on.

I had already packed for my trip, so I was ready to go when Tuesday morning came. Sherwood brought me to the airport. I was sad to leave him. It felt like I hadn't had much time for him since the day we got the news and had to cancel the wedding. But Sherwood's a trooper, always the supportive husband and father. He was with us every step of the way, doing whatever he could to make what he could easier for us. True to form, he was excited for both Kyle and me to be taking this trip together.

Until I hit my seat in the airplane I didn't realize how much stress I had been under. I went to sleep and struggled to wake up when I landed to change flights, the same happened on the second leg of my trip. I felt groggy still when I arrived in LA.

I turned on my cell phone to learn I had three voicemail messages waiting. One was Kyle telling me she was almost at the airport and where to meet her. The second one was from Sherwood; we had just received an offer on the house. I wasn't sure I heard him right. An offer already? We had just put it on the market a week ago. The market was in a downturn. We had been sure we'd be spending the winter in Pennsylvania.

So, with me on a bench in the LA airport and Sherwood at the lake in Vermont we agreed to accept the offer. The third call was the realtor wanting to know our decision. I called him back and said OK. Suddenly the stress was back!

I'm headed to Tahiti. I'm going to be gone for ten days. When I get back I'll have just five weeks to pack up and move out of the house. Oops – we have no place to move to. Our cottage would be closing for the season at about the same time. When it rains it pours.

I found a fax machine, papers came from PA, and I signed and returned them. I also made one phone call.

I believe in premonitions. In August, when I lost my job, we had looked at a beautiful piece of land on the lake. Not knowing for sure if we were ultimately going to move back to Vermont or not, we wanted to have some options.

Fortunately when we returned to Vermont in September we spoke with the land owner again and let him know that we definitely were moving back – once we sold our home. He had mentioned he was trying to sell his mother's house – but wasn't having any luck, and he might be interested in renting it. I have no idea why, but I did take the time to go and see it "just in case". It was a big house, in an older neighborhood, that had been well maintained.

I gave him a call, and he was interested in renting it out for six months! That would give us plenty of time to settle into the area and either find a house to buy, or build on his land if we chose to go in that direction.

I called Sherwood to bring him up to date. He's a bit of a Nervous Nellie so he was relieved to learn that I had managed to get the papers signed, returned, and secure a rental house since we had last spoken. His job while I was gone was to get moving boxes, and start boxing up non-household things like his tools.

Sometime it's amazing what you can accomplish in a short time when you have to.

I went to where I was supposed to meet Kyle. My cell phone rang, and she said she was at the curb. Then there she was. I was so happy to see her.

We ran to meet each other, hugged, and then I said you'll never guess what just happened to me!

Chapter XIII

KYLE

Finally it was time to take the trip to Tahiti. I was so happy that my mother had agreed to go with me. I knew that we would have a great time, but I also knew that she would understand my moods and give me space if I needed it.

As my friends pulled up to the curb to leave me off, I called my mothers cell phone. She'd be waiting inside. Just as promised – there she was. Although we'd just been together in Vermont it was great to see her.

Typical of our time together – one of us has a story to tell. We had no sooner finished our hug when she said, "you'll never guess what just happened to me!" It was just one more crazy turn to our story. We both stood there and just laughed.

I checked in, and Mom waited for me. Once we got through security we began talking about what she and Dad would do now. Why wasn't I surprised that she already had a plan!

We gave Dad a call to say good-bye one last time before we boarded. On the plane we settled in for a very long flight. We wouldn't arrive in Tahiti until late that evening.

PATTY

Kyle seemed relaxed and relatively happy. I know she had really been looking forward to this trip. I would make sure that whatever she wanted to do, we would do! She'd been through a lot over the last six weeks.

On the plane we visited, we read, we ate, and we slept. Fortunately the time went quickly.

Over the years we've traveled together a lot. This was the first time that she was responsible for all of the planning, and had taken care of the expense of rooms and connecting flights. I'd pick up the rest. I said a little thank you prayer for the nice severance package!

KYLE

We landed in Tahiti and took a cab to our hotel. I was holding my breath that it would be nice. It was! The first thing we did when we got in the room was order a late dinner. It was the beginning of our eating and drinking routine.

It was difficult to settle down to sleep. We were both excited to be there. But, we had another flight in the morning. We were going to Moorea.

Morning came and Mom was up before me. She had showered and it was my turn. We had a leisurely breakfast and went to the airport.

The small plane took us on a short flight to our next destination. In minutes we were at our hotel.

I loved the Tahitian way of greeting you with a cocktail. We had a fruity rum drink while we waited to be checked in and shown to our bungalow. I couldn't have been happier. It was perfect, right on the water with a nice deck out front.

We didn't sit still for long. We quickly got into our bathing suits to hit the beach. The water was the most amazing blue I had ever seen. We selected lounge chairs, and placed them at the edge of the water, this began our sunbathing ritual.

The resort was fantastic. We enjoyed sun filled days, lunches at the beach, and dinners on-site. As a special treat we spent a day horseback riding. This is a tradition Mom and I have had over the years. We both love horses and have been riding together everywhere from St. John in the Virgin Islands to Horseshoe Bend Arkansas – and everywhere in between. We weren't disappointed – the scenery was beautiful.

The time flew by and four days had passed in no time.

Now we are headed to Bora Bora.

PATTY

I loved the hotel in Tahiti, but was even more excited when we got to Moorea! I had only seen pictures of straw bungalows, and it was fun to be in one. We were right on the water, and it was beautiful.

I was so happy I had chosen to come. I had been reading a book called, *Inc. Your Dreams*. It was written by Rebecca Maddox, whom I had met. Her book walks you through the thought process of building a business. It was written with women in mind. I loved it. Kyle had given me a journal, and I had begun writing my thoughts and forming my long range business plan. When I finished the book, Kyle started reading it. It was time for her to decide what she'd really like to do with her life.

The process helped us both identify the things in life that were important to us. We did every exercise that was outlined. Of course at the time we didn't know if we'd ever bring our ideas to fruition but the process was therapeutic.

Evenings were the tough times for Kyle. This land of paradise was meant for couples and there wasn't a lot happening once you'd had dinner. This is when she should have been enjoying her "new husband." Instead she watched movies, played games, and visited with her "old mother."

She wore a brave face but I knew her heart was broken. How could it not have been?

KYLE

Bora Bora was also beautiful. Mom was happy – another grass bungalow! This one was on the beach but not as close to the water, but who could complain? The place was beautiful.

On this island we had planned to have massages and spend a day sailing and snorkeling. We also had a gift card to Bloody Mary's, a cool restaurant in town. Between lazy days on the beach and these extra activities it was bound to be great.

We began by sitting at the pool. Do you know how you can sense when someone is staring at you? Well, there was definitely a couple poolside that were giving us the eye. The next thing we know a bottle of wine was sent our way – a gift from the newlyweds. They had seen our story on one of the news shows. They wanted to let me know that they were proud of how I handled the situation. They were very sweet.

As bad as I was feeling, I'd look at Mom and continue to realize that the pain of our events really had an impact on a lot of people… her more than most. But, she taught me to be strong and always lead by example!

PATTY

Yeah – a grass bungalow!

We unpacked and went to the pool for lunch. We had decided, morning pool, afternoon at the ocean. It felt great to know that was the depth of the decision making we needed to make. Kyle and I were both drained and much more than that probably would have been too much.

At the pool Kyle received recognition for the first time from strangers. A newly married couple that had seen her story on TV sent us over a nice bottle of wine.

At every turn I was more impressed with Kyle than the day before! She thanked them and when they asked about her story, she shared. She didn't linger on the cancelled wedding but focused her story on the charity event held in its place. Listening to her was actually very inspiring.

The young bride had tears in her eyes as she related that she didn't know how she would have been able to handle it. Kyle simply told her that every situation is what you make it and we chose to make this one something better. Actually the bride wasn't the only one with tears in her eyes…

KYLE

Following lunch at the pool we went to the beach. We had a plan to follow after all.

We had been so fortunate that beautiful weather was with us day in and day out. We enjoyed the sun and more conversation. We planned dinner on the resort that evening and the next day we were going to go on a catamaran for an afternoon sail and snorkeling.

It was fun getting ready and going out to dinners. This evening we got table side seats to an amazing show as well, Tahitian dancers and beautiful songs.

Back at the room we did our own dance interpretation. I did pretty well I must say, but Mom had us in stitches...the moves she made were not meant for a woman in her mid 50's...and certainly not for a daughter to have to see. It was funny!

We thought we'd top the night off with a movie, if we could only get the TV to come in. A phone call to the service department was required. Our technician came, and eventually did get the set working for us. During the process we silently laughed thinking he should have been a plumber – if you know what I mean.

We selected movies that were light hearted, wanting to stay away from anything that would bring our moods down. It was a good call since even a comedy could get us crying!

PATTY

Our afternoon beach day was beautiful, but painful. There were several couples introducing themselves to each other and sharing stories of their weddings – of course they were all there on their honeymoons.

I saw Kyle take notice but without comment. I know my daughter, had she been there with her husband she would have been right in the middle of that group – the life of the party. She would have listened to all the stories but it would have been hers that would have captured the group's attention, and they would have organized some form of an outing or party for later. Instead she sat in the sun visiting with me. The people most drawn to speaking with us were a few older couples or single girls. Not quite the same mood.

We made the most of every minute. When she started to get down we would shop with the island vendors, order a fruity cocktail, or float in the ocean. It really was beautiful.

The next day it was breakfast in bed, the pool, a light lunch, and then onto the catamaran. It was just going to be us and of course, a newly wed couple. Our captain was new to the area but seemed like a great guy.

It was a gorgeous afternoon! We came to our first stop to snorkel. I was so excited, I hadn't been snorkeling in a few years and the water was gorgeous. We all got fitted with our gear, received our instructions and were in the water.

The coral, the fish, the water, everything was perfect. Kyle and I swam together. I was letting myself float for awhile admiring a school of fish when I realized I was drifting. I decided I'd better catch up with Kyle who'd swum ahead to another spot. I tried, and I tried, and I tried. I wasn't moving, I was in some sort of current. Oops – I might actually be in trouble. The boat was getting further and further away.

The captain had given an instruction that if we needed help at any point to raise our hand. So, I stopped trying to swim, began treading water, and waved my arm in the air. At last he noticed me and swam to me, I told him what was happening and he said to stay there, he was going to go bring the boat to me. He hadn't realized the strength of our current as I watched him struggle to get back to the boat.

Kyle yelled to me. She had seen my arm in the air was now concerned too – especially when she saw the captain trying to make it back on board the boat. I answered, and she started swimming to me. She yelled again, I answered, she kept coming. On the third yell I decided I was spent and had to save my energy so I didn't answer.

I actually kept remembering a story of two of my friends that went snorkeling as a cruise side trip. The husband ended up having a heart attack. He was in rough waters and panicked. So, with thoughts of him in my mind I was doing everything possible to just relax. And, I was kicking myself for not wearing a life preserver. Although not a strong swimmer I had never needed one before! Dang – I never may need one again if that Captain doesn't hurry up and get back to me.

Kyle got to me, as the Captain was just getting to the boat. As soon as she got there she realized what was happening – so together we treaded water and waited. Finally, he pulled up beside us and helped us on board. I was exhausted. I actually don't remember when I have ever been so physically spent! It took all I had to take off my gear.

The other couple was now waving to us, too. Although strong and experienced divers, they too had gotten caught up in the current and could not make it to the boat. So we swung around to rescue them. Sorry to say this, but I felt better knowing it wasn't just me!

KYLE

We were getting ready to go sailing – it was a perfect day to be on the ocean. I know that my mother loves snorkeling so I was also looking forward to that, more for her than for me. I'd be content to just sail. The water was gorgeous.

At our first stop the four of us got in and were instantly surrounded by beautiful fish. It was so relaxing. Mom and I were swimming together, and then we weren't. I surfaced to find her – she was just relaxing floating, looking at a school of fish. So, I went a little ways further enjoying myself as well.

A few minutes later I sensed something wasn't right. Where was my mother? Finally I see her with her arm waving in the air. That was our sign of distress that meant she needed help. I could see the Captain swimming to her. So I yelled, "Mom, are you OK?"

She quickly answered yes, but I knew I had to get to her. I yelled again, she answered. I swam further and realized I was in some sort of current and I wasn't making much progress getting to her. I yelled a third time – no answer. My heart was in my throat. This couldn't be happening. I couldn't bring my mother on my honeymoon and lose her. She couldn't be drowning!

I don't know where my strength came from but I used every ounce of energy I had to get to her. I started to yell at her for not answering me when she said she was sorry but needed to conserve energy...sure enough I knew what she meant. We were both treading water to stay afloat until the boat came to pick us up.

I was never so happy to see anyone as I was to see our Captain pulling up beside us and helping Mom on board. She looked pooped. I quickly got my equipment off and was at her side. But true to form, she was laughing at the situation we'd just been through and apologized for scaring me.

Although she laughed, we both new it really was no laughing matter. She really had come close to drowning, and I had come close to losing the most important person in my life. What a scare.

We had two more scheduled stops before heading back to the resort. When asked if she wanted to go back earlier of course she said no...she wouldn't want to ruin anyone's time. So, we kept on. At the next stop when the rest of us went in the water Mom chose to stay on the boat. That wasn't like her so I knew she was exhausted. But soon I looked back to see her taking pictures and I knew she was going to be fine. Relief!

PATTY

I must admit I was pretty happy to get back to the resort. When Kyle suggested a short nap before dinner I could have kissed her (actually I think I did). I was so tired. We slept!

I felt so much better when I woke up. Raring to go again, thank goodness…that had been a close call afternoon.

Tonight we are going by boat to a restaurant called Bloody Mary's. My sisters, Kathy and Jeanne, had given Kyle a gift certificate for her bridal shower. There was no sense letting it go to waste.

The restaurant was adorable, and the fresh fish was lined up on ice for you to select your entrée. We had a cocktail, ordered dinner, and talked about our day. It certainly made for exciting dinner conversation! We topped off the meal with dessert, and still not ready to call it quits we decided to sit at the bar until it was time for our boat to bring us back.

We met a nice young couple at the bar, on their honeymoon (surprise), visiting from New York. Kyle got in a conversation with them, and the next thing I knew it was three hours later and we were hurrying to catch the last boat to the island.

If I thought I was tired earlier in the day it was nothing compared to what I was feeling now – but it sounded nice to hear Kyle having such a good time and laughing with her new friends. So, I decided we'd stay as late as she wanted. Torture….

KYLE

What a great night! I loved Bloody Mary's! I loved being able to laugh at our day with Mom. Her reenactment had me in stitches. She really is such a good sport. But we both had to admit it had been scary and once again laughter was just our way of dealing with what might have been.

When dinner was over we had time before the boat would be there so we opted for a cocktail while we waited. We each ordered a glass of wine. A couple from New York sat beside us. Within seconds we had struck up a friendship. We enjoyed the evening having drinks, sharing stories, and laughing with them. In the end we had missed "several" boats back to the island!

Chapter XIV

KYLE

We slept-in the next morning and woke to our first and only day of rain. Not a problem, it was our spa day! We had massages scheduled for the morning and following that we were going shopping. I wanted to find some art and Mom wanted a black Tahitian pearl ring as a memory from our trip and to fill the bare spot on her finger.

I on the other hand have a beautiful blue diamond on my finger – where my engagement ring had been. The ring had special meaning. My Dad bought it for my mother when she was in St. John. It was a gift for their 20th anniversary. She loved it because it reminded her of the beautiful blue oceans in St. John, and of course made her think of Keith and Me who had been living there at the time for five years.

When my wedding was cancelled, I took off my engagement ring. As a surprise, my mother had her ring resized to fit me. It was a special gift now - from her to me. I was so happy when she told me what she had done, I loved the ring and knew it would be mine one day – I just hadn't expected it so soon. We went together to the jewelers to pick it up. I was so excited!

My mother had shared my story with the owners of the jewelry store, an older couple that had been married for many years. They had been touched by the story and the gift. They were so sweet to us. I think they were as excited as we were.

The store owner handed me the ring. I handed it to my mother and jokingly said, "You do the honors!" Without skipping a beat Mom took the ring put it on my finger and said, "With this ring I give you strength." The two of us laughed until we noticed the store owners hugging each other and crying as they watched. It really was quite special. A picture of me with my new ring ended up on the front page of our local paper the day after our event with my story.

The ring would always be special to me now, and I actually believed it would give me strength!

I really wanted to help Mom find a great replacement.

PATTY

I loved the spa – it was located in a tree house straw hut. It was so unique.

I didn't realize how tense I was until my technician began working my muscles. All the tension of the weeks leading up to this just seemed to melt away. When Kyle and I met after our treatments she described her experience exactly the same way. Needless to say, it was just what we needed.

Lunch and shopping followed. Kyle had success. She found two amazing pictures, one of a beautiful young Tahitian girl, the other of a young boy. I wasn't so lucky. Although there were a lot of lovely pearls, nothing quite matched what I was looking for. I decided I might just have to wait until we were headed back to the airport on our way home.

We had seen a store there that had a great selection – we just hadn't had the time to really look.

By the time we got back to the hotel the weather had cleared so we enjoyed a few hours at the pool before getting ready for our last night in Tahiti.

KYLE

Dinner was great. We ate on property, shared a wonderful bottle of wine, and talked about our travels and what was next for us.

We both had a lot on our plate. Mom had to go home to begin work on her new contract, pack her house in Pennsylvania, and prepare for her move back to Vermont.

I had to get back to work. And besides that I had hundreds of thank-you notes to write. I wanted to thank everyone who had attended the event, and everyone who had contributed to our charities.

Usually when I'm getting ready to leave my mother I start feeling down, but we had spent 10 great days together and we would be seeing each other in just three more weeks. The circumstances of which were going to be kind of weird.

To start, we would be meeting in New York City. We were invited to be special guests of a group of New York City special contributors for CARE. This would be followed by a spot on the Today Show. Then we'd fly back to Vermont together for my cousin Misty's wedding. And if that weren't enough, we'd be going to Washington DC from there so I could speak at a fund raiser for CARE.

Misty's parents, Uncle Norm and Aunt Laurie, had given me two round-trip airline tickets for a wedding present. Originally they were going to be used by me and my new husband, now they were going to be used by me and a guest. It was going to be difficult going to Misty's wedding. As happy as I was for her, I was afraid I was going to be really sad for me. So to help me through it my "guest" was going to be Jon. It was my way of saying "thank you" for all he had done, and I knew that having him with me would change the dynamic of conversations – hopefully people would be more comfortable with me there because I wouldn't be alone and mourning. I'd be with a friend having fun. At least that was the plan!

My parents were also anxious to meet Jon. We would spend an evening at the cottage, go to dinner, and then to the wedding the following day.

Needless to say, I began preparing myself mentally for what I knew would be more stress ahead!

PATTY

The final night of our honeymoon trip was wonderful. You'd think we would have run out of things to talk about, but per our usual, that simply wasn't the case.

At dinner we talked about what would happen when we got home. We had so much ahead of us.

I spoke with my husband each day, although briefly, and during each call we would make a list of "to do's" for him. His main job had been to get estimates from movers. They should be there when I got back.

I had set-up my home office before I left. I had purchased a new computer and printer, and was ready to get my teeth into my first consulting job. I wanted to be sure that moving didn't distract me from doing a great job for my client. After all, this first project would set the tone for moving forward.

I had also promised Kyle I'd be with her for two nights in New York. As I've said, she never ceases to amaze me – she's going to be on the Today Show and doesn't seem to be the least bit nervous. In fact she is more concerned over what she'll wear than what she'll say! You can't go to New York without shopping so I'm sure we'll be spending sometime in the stores. Note to self: pack comfortable shoes.

KYLE

We'll be taking the red eye home, so not to waste a moment, our morning was spent on the beach getting the last of the beautiful sun. It felt good.

Mom is all talk today about moving back to Vermont. Although we had talked about it throughout the week you could tell the difference today, she was getting anxious. She was so happy to have sold the house so quickly, although I know that added a whole new level of stress, and she was happy they would be back closer to family. Especially McKenna!

I'm a little sad about getting back to San Diego. I love it there. But if things had gone as planned I would have been coming back from my honeymoon and getting ready for a move of my own. Kurt and I were going to be moving east. Instead I'll be going back to living with a girlfriend, whom I love dearly, but it just wasn't the plan I had been looking forward to for so long.

Hopefully, financially, I will be able to get a place of my own in the spring. When I do I have some great art for the walls! I had the two pieces I purchased in Tahiti, as well as an amazing framed photo of a CARE project participant, representing the women who CARE works with. I love it.

We are heading to the airport a little early. We still have some shopping left to do!

PATTY

I found the ring, a black Tahitian pearl with diamonds on each side. When it fit perfectly I knew it was meant to be.

Now we were ready for the long trip home. On the plane our goal was to sleep. It didn't come as easy as we would have hoped but morning eventually came and we landed in Los Angeles.

Kyle and I said goodbye. She had friends picking her up for the drive back to San Diego and I had another flight to catch for Pennsylvania. We had just experienced a wonderful honeymoon together. Not many mothers and daughters can say that!

When I got to the airport Sherwood was waiting for me. It was great to see him. Picking me up had been a chore for him. He hated driving on the Philadelphia freeways. As he often reminded me, he's just a country boy!

KYLE

Sad to see my mother leave, but happy I'd be seeing her in just a few weeks. My friends were waiting and they all wanted to hear all about my trip!

If I thought my life would quiet down some when I returned I was wrong. I returned to 100's of emails from around the world, more offers to go on talk shows, and additional dollars were being donated to both charities in my honor. It was all quite humbling.

I hadn't seen people at work since the event. Evidently LaCosta had also been experiencing a barrage of emails and phone calls. People that wanted to reach me, or talk to them about me. I was so touched by some of the members who contacted me personally to tell me how proud they were of me. It was great to be able to have such a positive outcome to share with others.

PATTY

An interesting letter was waiting for me at home. Kurt had written to personally apologize for all the hurt we were experiencing because of him. He assured us he truly loved Kyle and simply had made some stupid mistakes. He also apologized about the expense of the wedding, and hoped that someday he would be in a position to repay us. It was a very sad letter from a young man who would live with the weight of his mistake for a long, long time.

When I called Kyle to tell her about the letter she said that she had one too. The difference being she threw hers away without ever opening it. In her mind there was nothing more she wanted to hear from him. It was time to put what could have been behind her.

I called the Vermont Children's Aid Society. When they learned I was moving back to Vermont they asked me to be on their Board of Directors. I wanted to continue being involved with the organization so naturally I agreed.

They also shared with me stories of people who had called, donated, or sent messages as the result of hearing Kyle's story. One touched me more than most. A young couple had recently lost their 18 month old child. They wanted to find a way to pay tribute to her. Kyle's story had inspired them. The mother said that she had loved the connection that Kyle and I had, and she loved the strength that Kyle had shown. This is what she would have hoped for her own daughter. So in her daughter's memory she requested that family and friends make donations to the Vermont Children's Aid Society.

So sad, and so sweat.

KYLE

I had been told there were emails waiting for me, but I had no idea. It would take me days to read through them all – there were 100's. Surprisingly they were from young women, mothers, and as many men.

To share a few –

Kyle, I am also a jilted bride that learned her fiancé was cheating. I am so proud to hear what you have done to turn your situation around and I wish I could attend your event. I just want to tell you how strong you are and a great role model for other women. Remember, there is someone so much better out there for you and you will find him. In the meantime, have fun being single:) My hat goes off to you. MF

Ms. Paxman: I'm a published novelist and live on an island near Seattle. Forget about the jerk! I'd marry you in a San Diego minute! VP

Kyle, you and your family are to be commended for setting such a fine example of turning bad news (is it really!?) into a worthy experience. Bravo!

I have no doubt you will recover from this development and lesson in your life and become stronger and wiser as a result. GWB

Dear Kyle, Congratulations! You are some kind of woman to turn your lemons into lemonade like you plan to do with your charity event. I am sure your heart is heavy, but perhaps all those other women, plus the help you'll be giving to others, will carry you through. You're an outstanding example to every other young woman who faces the same disappointment. I wish you well. AC

Dear Ms. Paxman, I just read about your benefit (previously wedding) in the New York Times. Talk about making lemonade! I'm really impressed by how you managed to bounce back from a cancelled wedding to think of something both creative and worthwhile.

All the best – which often does arise from circumstances beyond our control. DV

Dear Ms. Paxman, I read your story on AOL and all I have to say is "YOU GO GIRL!!!!" You turned a horrible situation into a positive event. I really don't think you will have trouble finding a date after this. You are a very pretty and more importantly you have a huge caring heart. MC

Ms. Paxman, I read about your charity event in Vermont and I had to email and tell you what special people you and your Mom are. My daughter is getting married next year and I hope we would have the vision and unselfishness to create such a positive outcome to what could have been such a difficult time. You are young and it is clear that your life will be a wonderful love story for you. But the wonderful reality is that the love story already exists for you now, with all the people you have touched by your generosity and ingenuity, and this is something that that is not achieved by everyone in their lifetime. Cheers! CD

It was so heartwarming to realize I really had made an impact and touched so many lives with my story. Do I wish the outcome had been different? Absolutely! But I am proud of how I dealt with everything – and I will find a way to continue making a difference.

Kyle boarding the flight to Moorea

Kyle and Patty enjoying dinner in Moorea

Kyle sailing in Bora Bora

Kyle and Patty horseback riding in Moorea

Chapter XV

PATTY

The weeks have flown by for me. I can't believe it is time to head to New York to meet Kyle. To say I had been busy since returning from Tahiti would be an understatement. I worked on my new consulting assignment with vigor and was receiving rave reviews from my clients. Sherwood and I had nearly finished packing our house and were scheduled to move at the end of the month. And, daily I spoke to Kyle.

I wish I could say she seemed happy and life was back to normal for her, but that wasn't the case. She is doing her best but at every turn she is being reminded of all that happened. New articles are being written about her, on-line bloggers are going crazy sharing their opinions, and she continues to get asked to be on TV and radio shows.

I think she is making the right decision to pass on all of these, with the exception of the commitments she has already made. I know she would like to continue being a spokesperson for the charities but what no one else seems to get, every time she says "yes" it is costing her time and money. She really just can't afford it right now.

As I continue to communicate with the Vermont Children's Aid Society we have learned how they plan to spend the money Kyle raised for them. They will fund the development of a Kids-A-Part Program. The program is designed to help children of incarcerated parents, which is nationally a significant issue. When a parent goes to prison children pay a price. They lose a parent, or in the case of a single parent, their entire family. This either puts them into the foster system or living with a relative, usually a grandparent. It will be interesting to be involved with helping this program to fruition.

KYLE

Life for me has been a bit tough. I've been working, returning email messages, writing thank you notes, and working with CARE to select where my funds will be spent. Trying to heal through the process didn't seem to be happening for me. But I moved on.

I chose to have my donation go to Bolivia, and if all goes as planned I will travel with CARE to Bolivia in the spring. I really want to experience firsthand the difference a little bit of money can make to a third world country.

In Bolivia the average age life expectancy of a man is 32 years old. Many men work in the mines and die young from mining accidents or black lung disease. When a husband dies the wife sends the son into the mine to support the family and the cycle continues. CARE has built schools to teach trades to women, helping them become self supportive by learning a vocation. My dollars will go towards this effort. $10,000 can bring power and water to a school; it can pay for supplies and teachers. I feel confident that CARE will use it the best way possible.

Most people, when they hear of the hardships being experienced in other countries, react by sending "what is needed" in the form of clothes, supplies, etc. CARE does not support this type of help – they believe it is far more important to teach people how to be self sufficient.

Giving them what they need doesn't solve the problem. It simply serves as a band aid.

I'm excited to know that I can have a significant impact, not just today, but for generations to come.

The General Manager at LaCosta called me into his office to tell me how proud he was of me. He wanted to do something, to give something, to show his support. I was blown away when he offered to pay for my flight to Bolivia. What a generous gift. It was so thoughtful that it made me cry.

The next few weeks were very hard. I was struggling with my personal life. I was sad much of the time. A beautiful honeymoon and a wonderful charity, while a good distraction for a couple of weeks, couldn't take away the pain and hurt of all that had happened. It had been good medicine, but it hadn't been a cure. I was grateful for my friends, who continued to be caring and supportive. I knew that time could eventually heal all wounds but getting to that point was painful. I wanted time to pass quickly. I was ready to move on.

PATTY

Sherwood left for Vermont and I left for the airport. I was flying to New York to meet Kyle. It would be good to see her again. We had been talking back and forth about all that was happening this week.

We were going to meet at the airport and take a cab into Manhattan together. I was anxiously pacing at baggage claim waiting for her.

I was so happy when I finally saw her. As always she looked beautiful, but a bit thin. I was hoping she would have put some of the weight back on she'd lost over the past two months.

We hugged and went to catch a cab. The conversations began!

KYLE

I was anxious to see Mom again, and happy to be in New York. I always loved the fast pace and energy of the city.

Mom was waiting for me with open arms. I couldn't wait to tell her about work, CARE, and life in general. We had plenty of time – the traffic was horrendous.

At the hotel we were meeting with two people from CARE. Together we would be going to dinner and then to a cocktail reception being hosted by the New York Bolivia special contributors.

We met some amazing advocates. These were people whose ordinary lives were very different than ours – as was easy to see from the penthouse apartment overlooking Central Park. We also found there was a lot of commonality. We were all passionate about helping others. Some in attendance had personally visited Bolivia and were able to share stories with us that were inspiring.

The next day we would be going to the Today Show. Matt Lauer was originally going to be the person interviewing me, but a small plane had crashed into a downtown apartment building that day and he was now covering this sad story.

In the morning Mom and I went to the NBC Studio with the PR person from CARE. I would be following Jimmy Buffet – Mom's a fan so she was pretty stoked about that!

We waited in the Green Room with other guests as we watched the show being filmed.

PATTY

We are dressed and ready to go – Kyle opted for a casual outfit that was adorable on her.

On our way into the Green Room we said hello to Al and Meredith. The Green Room was not nearly as glamorous as we had expected. It was basically a waiting area with pastries. Actually really good pastries!

They came to get Kyle and she was off to hair and makeup. While she was gone Matt stopped in for a donut before he took off to do his live reporting at the sight of the plane accident.

Kyle came back and it was soon her turn. We went back stage and watched Jimmy Buffet perform. He was great! When he was finished he walked by us, shook our hands and said hi. It was crowded back stage. There certainly was a lot of activity behind the scenes.

The show went to commercial, Kyle was moved to the couch on stage, and I went back to the Green Room to watch her on TV.

The film they had recorded in advance, from California, was great. Kyle handled the interview questions with ease. I was so proud of her. She had been told the type of questions she'd be asked in advance of the live show. The reporter must not have had the same person prepping her as she seemed more interested in the relationship than the charity event. I was impressed with the way Kyle turned the interview around to talk about the event and how the work with the two charities had transformed both of us. She shared how I was now working with Vermont Children's Aid Society and was serving on their Board of Directors, and that she would be going to Bolivia with CARE.

When did she become such a poised public speaker?

KYLE

Prep, hair, make-up, action! It all seemed to move so quickly. I was sitting on the couch waiting to be interviewed and then it was over – I couldn't remember what I was asked. I couldn't remember how I answered. I could remember being surprised with the questions, thinking let's talk about the charities – but that was it.

When I came back to the Green Room the people there cheered and told me I did a great job – of course my biggest fan, Mom, was beaming. She thought I did great too, in fact she said I did better than the person interviewing me. It's always nice to get that level of support.

People were recording the show for us, so I know at some point in the future I will watch the tape. In the meantime I can only hope I was half way decent. My phone seemed to ring nonstop for the remainder of the day with friends and family calling to say they'd seen me and to let me know they thought I had done well.

For me the best part was that it was over with, one less thing to worry about. I was ready to go shopping. I was going to get a new dress for the wedding the one I was originally going to wear was now too big. We spent all day shopping and went to a little pub for dinner, one that a friend had suggested.

As we were enjoying dinner we noticed a young man watching us from the bar. He came over, bought us a drink, and told us he had seen us on the Today Show. He told me I was inspirational and that he had been really impressed with me and Mom. The attention was a little embarrassing. His gesture was thoughtful.

PATTY

In the morning we flew to Vermont and Sherwood was there to pick us up at the airport. We went to the cottage where we would stay for the next two nights. I love being on the lake and this trip was no exception.

Sherwood was so proud of Kyle. I loved hearing him tell her how he felt as he was watching her.

The next afternoon Kyle went to pick up Jon. We anxiously waited to meet our hero. He was a little bashful when he first arrived, understandably so. That evening the four of us went out to dinner and had a wonderful time. It was interesting hearing the story from his perspective. He was torn bringing her the news, but he knew he would have wanted someone to tell him if the situation had been reversed.

Sherwood and I went to bed when we got back to the cottage, and the kids stayed up to visit. It was so good to hear the laughter. It was quite late before they said good night.

The next day was Misty's wedding. We moved from the cottage to the hotel near where the wedding was being held. Kyle was going to show Jon around Burlington, they'd meet us in the lobby later.

As we were getting dressed to go to the ceremony I was starting to feel a little sad.

KYLE

I wasn't surprised that Jon and my parents hit it off so nicely. They visited like they had known each other forever. Before leaving the cottage Jon wrote a note in their journal thanking them for having him and expressing his admiration for our family for turning lemons into lemonade.

We had a fun afternoon in Burlington. After we dressed and met for the wedding, I have to say he looked hot! I expected him to be nervous meeting the rest of my family but if he was it never showed. One person after another thanked him for not only telling me the bad news, but helping me deal with it throughout the process. If he'd ever questioned his decision he wouldn't have after meeting my family.

I don't know how I would have made it through Misty's wedding without Jon. We had a blast. Keith, Julia, Mom, Dad, Me, Jon and my

Aunt's best friends shared a table. The meal was wonderful, the band was great, and we danced and visited all night long. I was so happy for Misty and so happy for me that I wasn't at all sad.

I wasn't as sure about my mother.

PATTY

So far so good – the wedding was beautiful and very touching. Misty and Chris looked so happy. I loved seeing my brother Norm walk her down the aisle. He was definitely a proud father.

I thought I was fine until we went through the receiving line. I don't know what happened but when I hugged Misty it took all I had in me to hold it together. I went from the receiving line to the ladies room. In my own private little stall I sobbed uncontrollably for what seemed like an awfully long time. I don't know where all those emotions had been hiding but they sure found their way out all of a sudden. Now to go back out and appear normal… breathe deep. I can do this!

The party was in full swing and no one seemed to notice I had been missing, or if they did, they were being kind and not mentioning it. The rest of the evening was fine, it actually turned out to be far more fun than I expected. After all it was a celebration.

KYLE

After the wedding reception the party continued back at the hotel. My brother and sister-in-law, Aunts, Uncles, and friends closed the place down. Absent from the crowd were my parents. I felt badly because I knew my mother was probably having a tough time with the whole wedding scene – but she stayed strong and made it through the night with no one the wiser.

I will admit, I had a few more cocktails than I should have. The next morning I was one of the last to arrive for breakfast. Jon and I were going to go to Keith's for the next night, and then early flights to catch on Monday. Jon was going back to San Diego, Mom and I would be off to Washington DC where I was going to speak at the 61st Anniversary Celebration for CARE. Dad was driving back to Pennsylvania.

The CARE event was at the historic Willard Hotel. The reception served as an opportunity to honor those who have worked tirelessly to promote CARE's mission, helping raise funds that fight poverty and promote dignity around the world.

Dr. Helene Gayle spoke with deep appreciation for the efforts of so many. The room was filled with over 100 CARE friends from diplomatic, corporate and civic communities. Dr. Gayle remarked upon the importance of fighting poverty through empowering woman and girls, stating unequivocally that, "If we invest, if we act, if we utilize our collective power – we can empower women, their families, and their communities around the world." This is the essence of CARE's mission.

Guest included Empress Farah Pahlavi of Iran; Ambassador and Mrs. Ferguson of New Zealand; and officials from the Indonesian, South African, French and Canadian embassies; as well as friends and supporters. I felt honored to be among them.

PATTY

The CARE celebration was a special moment for Kyle and me. It was so nice to meet so many people that supported this great cause.

The most poignant moment of the evening came with the story shared by Kyle. She closed the evening's program with an inspiring story of empowerment. Having cancelled her wedding because of an unfaithful fiancé, she shared how she decided to use her would-be wedding reception as an opportunity to unite strong women around a charitable cause. After seeing a commercial for CARE she designated the organization as a recipient of money raised.

In an unwavering voice of strength and character she told the group that "breaking her heart actually opened it up to others." She further added, "I have been touched by this organization and will do whatever I can to encourage others to get involved – whether it is by making a contribution to CARE, or talking to friends, or talking to our legislators about the power they have to change people's lives around the world."

Not surprisingly, guest were moved, many coming up to Kyle to thank her for her story, for her generosity, and for her courage.

Chapter XVI

PATTY

Sherwood and I were getting ready to move back to Vermont. A few more days and we'd be saying good-bye to Pennsylvania. We had a good run, but now we were anxious to go home! Nothing beats being near family, we had really missed having that closeness during the seven and one half years we were away.

Today, however I'm anxiously waiting to hear from Kyle. She is going to Los Angles to tape the Ellen Show. I knew what time she was taping, so I waited by the phone. No call. Then Keith called to see if I had heard from Kyle. Evidently he had. She was not happy at all.

The reason she had picked the Ellen Show was because of the theme: to acknowledge ordinary people that did extraordinary things. She was told that Ellen had heard her story and asked personally to have her on the show. Kyle's expectation was that the focus of the interview would be on the event and the charities. Like her last interview, however, there was apparently more interest in the detail behind the news of the broken engagement. So, according to Keith, Kyle was really disappointed.

The fact that I hadn't heard from her was disturbing. She was going to call me. I was so worried, I was afraid she was really upset. The more time that went by the more nervous I got. I kept leaving messages. Why wasn't she answering her cell phone?

It was the next morning before I heard from her. My sleepless night was for naught. Although she had been disappointed in the interview she had just had one of the "most fun" nights ever with her friends in LA. What a relief! Although I was a bit miffed she hadn't called I was happier that she was having fun.

That afternoon Sherwood and I watched the Ellen Show together. The pre-shots and story lines that were shown throughout the first half of the show, prior to commercials, were great. They showed the event and highlighted the story. There she was – walking on to the stage – dancing to Ellen's tunes as she moved to the couch. She was wearing a CARE tee shirt "I am powerful." Too cute for words!

The interview was short, but it was good. She did a nice job. We were proud of her. At the end of the interview Ellen gave her a $1,000 gift certificate to Bed Bath and Beyond. Kyle whispered something to her which we couldn't really make out, and Ellen told her she was sweet.

Our phone began ringing immediately – evidently a lot of other people had been watching too!

KYLE

I went to LA with my best friend from college, Adam, and his girlfriend. They had both been with me in Vermont during my charity event. My Matron of Honor, Jess, was also with me, and the PR person from Care.

Adam and his girlfriend were in the audience. Jess and the PR person were waiting in the Green Room. Jess was enjoying the mini bar!

I was taken to a pre-interview. It was obvious that the questions they wanted to ask were not relevant to the charities or the event as I had anticipated. They were far more interested in everything that led up to that point. I would do my best to mention both charities. I was so thankful I had worn my care "I am powerful" tee shirt.

It was my turn. I'm ready. This time when the filming is over I'm going to remember what I said during the interview. I was so glad that I had friends with me providing their support. I followed Kathryn Heigel.

There was a pre-tape and then I was introduced. I danced out onto the stage and there I was with Ellen DeGeneres. The questions did disappoint me. I really wanted to focus on the charities – but evidently the idea of a cheating fiancé was more interesting. I did my best to push the conversation so that I could mention both of the charities and talk about the end result.

The time went quickly. As Ellen was saying good-bye to me she presented me with a gift certificate for $1,000 – to help me when I moved into my own apartment again. The gift was thoughtful, but I asked her, can we give this to the charities? She laughed and told me I was sweet. Segment over.

I met my friends afterwards and they were excited. They thought I'd done a nice job. I wasn't happy. Keith called and I told him as much. After that I wasn't in the mood to talk to anyone, so I shut off my phone. I'll call my mother in awhile.

As it turned out I didn't get that call in until morning. I felt bad later. There must have been six or seven voice messages from Mom. The last few sounded a little panicked. I should have called her. My friends and I had gone out to enjoy LA. We ate, we drank, we danced, and I even road the bull in Hollywood. It was more fun than I had experienced in months!

I knew Mom was upset with me despite trying her best not to sound it. After she saw the show we talked again and she assured me I was much better than I had given myself credit for.

PATTY

Our move to Vermont went off without a hitch. It was October 31st – Halloween when we moved into our rental house. We worked all day watching the movers unload trucks and I spent my time directing where everything would go. I couldn't believe that in the middle of an obvious move, kids in costumes started ringing our doorbell trick-or-treating. I had one small box of candy bars, some granola bars, and some snack bags of potato chips. I shut the lights out but they kept coming. I was really hating Halloween – feeling a little witchy!

Within two days, typical of our moving style, the house looked like we had been in it for years. It was going to serve us well until we found the house we wanted to buy. I was back in business and again focused on my contract.

It soon became apparent to me that something was amiss with the company I was working for. The man that was in charge of reviewing and signing off on my projects was not answering my emails. I wasn't getting any feedback on the work I was submitting. It took several weeks before I learned what was wrong. Evidently the President of the company and a few of his key people had decided to leave the organization. What the heck? It was mid November – and I was contracted through December. But what do you do when something like this happens? I had no idea since I was new to the whole consulting thing. Our contract was not much more than a hand shake.

I learned a few good business lessons! Fortunately the President was a man of integrity – he was willing to pay me for the remainder of the year. I didn't feel comfortable getting paid to do work that was not going to be used, so we ended our agreement in November.

Now I was a consultant with no business in front of me! I spent the next two months writing my business plan, developing my brochure and business cards, and then launched my first marketing campaign. I wrote a letter introducing my company and services to people that I knew within the industry. My first mailing went to 20 people. I would do small mailings, 20 at a time. At least that was the plan. 20 people, 20 follow-up phone calls. To my great surprise, that first campaign; that first mailing netted me 10 clients. I was back in business, and so my business went on, and grew.

I was asked to speak at the Vermont Children's Aid Society's Annual Banquet and share Kyle's story. I was happy to. The money she had raised for them was indeed making a difference as they shared at the banquet a new program being developed to help children – Kids-a-part. They also surprised me by creating an Award. It was the Kyle Paxman – Women Make a Difference annual award. I was deeply touched, as was Kyle when I shared the news with her. The first woman to receive it was in fact a mother who had been incarcerated. She and her children had already benefited from the new program.

Although the recipient had made some bad decisions in her life she recognized the importance of doing what was right. To give her children a better life, one that she couldn't provide for them, she found the strength to allow her children to be adopted by a caring and loving family. The Kids-a-part program helped her and her children through the difficult transition. Her story was one of many that would benefit from the contribution we had made to Vermont Children's Aid. I was glad I had made a commitment to be on their Board of Directors.

Life was going well. I loved being back in Vermont, I loved being my own boss, I loved chairing the Development Committee for Vermont

Children's Aid Society, and I was really loving being near family – especially McKenna. What a joy to see her growing up and developing her funny little personality. I kept thinking how lucky I was. I would have missed all of this if I hadn't lost my job! McKenna's first words were Pop Pop – which made Sherwood very happy.

The only thing missing was Kyle. We planned a trip to Las Vegas for early February.

KYLE

I was keeping busy with work, and I was seeing my new friend Jon regularly. Maybe if circumstances had been different he would have been more but we were both happy with the friend relationship.

I had hoped my story would have fizzled out but it seemed everywhere I went someone recognized me, or a friend of a friend wanted to hear all the details. It was difficult.

My former fiancée moved to the East Coast as we had originally planned to do together. I was really glad that he had left California. I no longer had to fear the prospect of running into him. I did have the occasion of running into the girl he had cheated with. It was an encounter I'm sure we'll both remember. I've often wondered if that Bloody Mary ever came out of her nice white shirt. Maybe I was a little impulsive and out of character, but it felt good!

I felt like my life had stood still. I wasn't going anywhere. I wasn't happy. Perhaps I needed to find something new in my life. A man I use to work with had moved to Caesar's Palace in Las Vegas. He was in charge of Food and Beverage. He wanted me to consider coming to work for him, managing one of their restaurants. I asked Mom if she wanted a few days away, and we could enjoy Vegas while I was there. I had never been. If nothing else we would have fun.

I loved Las Vegas but it was clear before I ever went to visit my friend that it was not my kind of town. That didn't stop Mom and me from having a good time. We toured the strip, had wonderful meals, and took in a show. We went to see Cirque du Soleil – Love – the Beatles. It was the perfect choice, Mom and I both knew every song and the show was spectacular.

My few days with Mom were over too soon. I was heading back to San Diego and feeling more depressed than I had been before I left. I had loved hearing all the latest stories of McKenna, how Keith and Julia were doing, the joys of house hunting, and of course Mom's job. I missed family.

My parents had planned a family vacation to St. John in May. My step brother and sister and their families, Keith, Julia, and McKenna were all invited to go. It would be wonderful and something else positive to look forward to. Three more months – I'd be fine until then.

PATTY

Typical of my time with Kyle – we had a lot of fun in Vegas. I was pretty relieved when she announced very quickly that it was not her kind of town. She did go through the motions with her friend, we were there after all, but she let him know she wasn't interested.

Our time together had been very upbeat, but when we parted I could still see that the old sparkle in Kyle was missing. She was like a lost soul. It was apparent that the events of the past year had taken quite a toll on her.

When "the call" came the following month, I wasn't surprised. Kyle had decided it would do her good to leave California and come back home for awhile. She would keep her job up until our family trip in

May. Immediately after that she would move home temporarily – until she felt ready to make the right decisions for her future.

I have to say we were all ecstatic. It would be great having her with us again. Sherwood and I had just found the new house we wanted and we would be settled in by the time she joined us.

The house was beautiful, at the end of a cul-de-sac, with a large fenced in back yard bordering the Winooski River. The lower level was unfinished – that was my next project before moving in. Now with Kyle coming home the design I had drawn was even more appropriate. The family room that opened to the pool and patio would have a custom bar; the bedroom would have a private sitting room and bathroom.

I wanted all work done before we moved in. We closed on the house and three weeks later the contractor had finished the lower level – it was beautiful. I bought new furniture and decorated in tones I knew Kyle would love. It came out even better than expected.

Soon the boxes started arriving with Kyle's things, she was sending a little bit at a time. I was hoping that with every box shipped she was feeling a little better.

KYLE

Calling home to ask if I could come back temporarily was difficult. I felt like I was too old for this, but on the other hand I knew I needed it. Of course my parents were thrilled. I had known they wanted me closer…maybe they hadn't planned on quite so close, but I knew they were happy with my decision.

Now I had a lot to do. I had to give notice at work, pack my stuff, ship it off to Vermont, and say good bye to all of my friends. I knew that would be the hardest, but I also knew that because they were true friends I would see them all again.

In fact, some of them planned a trip to St. John the same week as my family to coincide with my 30th birthday. We had lived together in St. John, and then in San Diego; they would have been in or at my wedding. I was touched that they decided to be a part of another important turning point in my life.

The next month flew by and I was headed to St. John! My parents rented Great Expectations, the same property we had when Keith and Julia got married there four years earlier.

It was good to be with family! We had a lot to celebrate – Mother's Day, my birthday, and Dad's birthday.

The beaches of St. John are beautiful we visited different ones each day. We saw old friends, enjoyed the local restaurants, and enjoyed each other.

The night of my 30th birthday we went to LaTapa, the restaurant I had once managed. Mom and Dad talked to Alex, the owner, and she had reserved the porch for us. It was more people than she would usually seat out there but she wanted us to have the best spot! We invited all of my friends - those that had traveled to St. John to join us – and a special friend Annie who still lived there.

The night started with a champagne toast. My godfather, Uncle Tom, had called ahead to place the order, my brother Keith made the toast. I was so touched I cried.

The dinner ended with another surprise. My friend Mark, who had lived with us in St. John, now in California, couldn't make the trip but he also sent a toast. We laughed – his was tequila shots for everyone. The night was perfect. Lots of laughter, lots of fun!

Another night that will always be special to me while in St. John was a simple BBQ at the house. Again, friends were invited to join us. I asked Annie, who was an artist, to bring some of her work. Her paintings were so amazing I knew people would be interested in buying them. I know I personally wanted to own one.

I'm not sure in total how much she sold that evening but I do know my mother bought four beautiful carnival pictures that would line the walls of my sitting room at the new house. Annie was so touched. She loved my parents and couldn't believe they would want her art in their house.

That evening and those photos would have more meaning than any of us could have imagined at the time. Poor Annie was tragically killed in an automobile accident less than a year later. That was the last time we saw her. Thank God for her beautiful art, in every picture we can see her heart. As we would talk about her in times to come it would always be about her strength and creativity. She was a strong woman who had made a difference! Losing her I knew would leave an empty spot in my heart forever.

PATTY

St. John was the perfect family trip. It was great to be together at a place we all love. The celebrations seemed endless. Saying good-bye to Kyle was easy – she would be moving back to Vermont the following week. I couldn't wait to show her the house, and especially her room.

When she arrived, her enthusiasm for the house was great. She loved it! It was so nice to have her home. She immediately jumped in and became part of the household again. Within days she found a job –she was hired to manage the bar at a local social club – the Ethan Allen Club.

Hopefully being home would help her heal. It was sad to realize what an impact her cancelled wedding had.

∽ Chapter XVII ∽

KYLE

A year has nearly passed since my canceled wedding I am shocked to realize that I haven't completely healed. I really needed to be home with family more than I realized. It was great to be part of the normal activities of family life. I was enjoying being with Keith and Julia and getting to be a part of McKenna's life. I enjoyed relaxing by the pool before going to work, and when I wasn't working, I enjoyed going to the cottage.

The one thing missing was a social life. I had no desire to date, and I had no interest in going out and partying. This was so unlike me. I hadn't been without a boyfriend for more than a short period of time since I was 15 years old. Now when I noticed someone taking "interest" in me I would distance myself. I just didn't need to get involved in a relationship. For now all I needed was time.

As the summer was coming to an end we planned a First Anniversary Event to create additional awareness for CARE and the Vermont Children's Aid Society. It would be held at the Ethan Allen Club where I worked. This time, my sisters and aunts were selling tickets to our event. We arranged speakers, music, and a silent auction. The two charities were thrilled to be a part of it. I was happy to again have the opportunity to make a difference as an advocate.

Mom and I both spoke, as did representatives from the two charities. It was surprising that there was still so much emotion in my mother's story – it always surprises me to hear her voice quiver, that doesn't happen often. She told the beginning of our story talking about everything that led us to this day. When I spoke I shared the impact of our donations to both organizations, and the difference we were able to make with their help.

The event went well and we raised an additional $12,000 for the charities. We found it a little more difficult this time around. We were charging for tickets, and our story was not as raw as it had been initially. Regardless, we knew that the money raised would be a great gift to our charities and would be put to good use. True to our theme – Women Make a Difference.

PATTY

I don't know if Kyle's heart was into having a First Anniversary Event. Did she really want to promote her pain again? We talked about it, and while she really did want to move on, she also wanted to continue supporting the charities. The First Anniversary Event would be one way she could again make a significant contribution. So the event was put into motion. Everyone had a good time, and it was a success.

That evening, after everything was over, Kyle and I had a champagne toast and ate the top of the cake from the first event! Neither of us had enjoyed it a year earlier – tonight we loved it. We laughed as we toasted our first anniversary eating year old cake and celebrating how far we both had come.

As we moved into winter I knew Kyle was getting restless. She hated the cold and in Vermont that is all there is in the winter – cold and snow! Although I knew she would make the most of it, I also knew she was ready to move on.

KYLE

I was prepared to try one more winter in Vermont. I was hoping I'd surprise myself and love it. That wasn't the case. I was dressed in layers all the time, and even then never felt warm. More than anything I hated wearing boots and parkas.

The holidays however were amazing. It was so nice to be with family and share in all the traditions I had been missing – everything from baking Christmas cookies, to going shopping with Dad for his gifts to Mom. We had pre-Christmas celebrations with friends and relatives, our Christmas Eve dinner out and a beautiful Christmas Day. We had our tree in the morning and spent the afternoon with Keith, Julia, McKenna and Julia's family. It was a special time, and there was much for all of us to give thanks for.

My Mom's family, the Burrington's, always have a big family Christmas Party. Eight kids, spouses, children, grandchildren – as you might imagine, there are a lot of us. This year Mom planned the party at the house. Rather than the normal Yankee Exchange, we adopted families in need. Having remained actively involved with the Vermont Children's Aid Society they identified three families with children that wouldn't be in a position to have much of a holiday without help. Names and wish lists were assigned. A big part of our party was spent wrapping the gifts and preparing them for delivery. We found another way to give back. Everyone loved it!

PATTY

Kyle and I have started talking about where she wants to live, and how she will decide. She doesn't want to go back to anywhere she's already been. She wants warm weather, and she definitely wants to be near the ocean. Her former boss in St. John had visited us in Vermont over the summer and talked about Key West, Florida. To her it felt like St. John but in the states. It became a place of interest for Kyle.

We started to plan a trip for January. It would be a nice break and give her a chance to check-it-out before making any decisions. On a business trip to St. Louis I had dinner with some old friends of mine who worked for a national corporate travel/planning organization. Tim said he was going to "hook us up!" and he did.

We stayed at the Westin, right on the water, in beautiful rooms, at a significantly discounted price. It was great. Tim knew Kyle and her work experience, so he also had put a phone call in to the General Manager, a friend of his. She wanted to meet Kyle while we were there.

KYLE

Mom and I flew into Miami and rented a car. We were driving to Key West. Mom had been to the Keys before on business trips, but it was my first visit. I wanted a warm location, check. I wanted more conveniences, and stores, than were available on St. John, check. I wanted smaller than San Diego, check. I needed beach, check. I wanted a fresh start, somewhere where I didn't feel like "that girl" and everyone didn't know my story, check. If I decided to move here I would need a job and a place to live. There was the hurdle!

Our first evening in town we had a great dinner out, lobsters my favorite food. The next day we went to the pool, shopped, and rode

156

around Key West to acquaint ourselves with the island. The next morning I had an appointment to speak with the General Manager. It wasn't a job interview, it was just a meeting. We had a nice conversation and she asked me a lot of questions.

I really liked her! She shared her story with me, what brought her to Key West, and she talked about what it was like living there. It all sounded very positive. It was clear that they didn't have any management opening at the Westin, but things can change quickly on resort properties, so she would definitely keep me in mind if anything did become available. I was happy with that, because the paper was full of job openings. I was confident I could find something if I decided this was going to be my place.

The next day as Mom and I were returning to our room from the pool the phone rang. The General Manager wanted to know if I had just a few minutes. She'd like me to meet the Food and Beverage Director. I explained I had just walked in the room, from the pool. I was told to throw on a cover up and come on down. So, I did.

Tom was in charge of F&B. He was also very nice. We hit it off quickly. Again I was told if anything opened up they'd keep me in mind.

The next day I was offered a full-time position as Food and Beverage Manager on their private island Sunset Key. I would be day manager in charge of their highest-end restaurant Latitude's, the Pool Café, pool service, beach service and room service. Needless to say I was shocked. The pay was good, the benefits were good, and they offered management housing, also good. I accepted the position and agreed to be there in early February.

I had found my new place! We called home that evening to share the news with Dad. He was so happy for me. Mom was beside herself, she was so proud.

PATTY

Kyle needed something positive in her life right now. She wanted someplace new. Offering her a management position one day, when the day before they didn't have any openings, was perfect. They had been impressed with her background, her knowledge, and her personality. They wouldn't regret their decision. She is great!

We celebrated that night over dinner, and began making plans for her move to Key West. She would have three more weeks at home before leaving. It was going to be hard for Sherwood and me to see her go. It had been a joy having her with us again. But we certainly understood her desire to get on with her life.

That evening when we got back to the room I called home. Sherwood had just had a bad day. He woke up to blood in his urine. As the day progressed so did the blood. He drove himself to the Emergency Room. He was told it might be a kidney infection. They gave him some medicine and scheduled additional tests for the next day. I was so upset. It had to have been bad for him to drive himself to the hospital. He assured me he was fine, and he was already feeling better from the medicine. When I told him we would come home a day early, he wouldn't hear of it - he would be fine. In the end he did agree to have someone go with him. I called Keith.

I spoke to Sherwood again in the morning before his appointment. Evidently the bleeding had become worse overnight, but he still remained calm. Not so with Keith. I spoke to him a few hours later and never heard such panic and concern. Sherwood was losing control of his urinary function – he was now urinating what appeared to be straight blood. He had already changed his clothes once. Keith was on his way back to the house for another outfit. It didn't sound good.

Not the way we wanted to end our trip. We couldn't get home fast enough.

If that wasn't enough we got another call, Kyle's Uncle Paul had fallen and was in the hospital in a coma. Our good news day had a horrible ending.

KYLE

Mom was really worried. I was really worried. Keith was well past being worried. He was panicked. Dad remained calm. Sherri came and organized the next appointments.

When we got home it was a relief just to see Dad. He told us what had happened. His test results showed tumors on his bladder. He had an appointment scheduled to see an urologist.

My Uncle was in ICU. I called my Aunt to find out how he was doing. She suggested that we come up to see him, and say our good-byes.

That is how Mom and I spent our first day home.

PATTY

Sherwood seemed calm when we went to the doctor's office. They were scheduling surgery for the week after Kyle was leaving. The tumors were going to be removed and would be tested for cancer. I realized they don't give you too much information early on. It's one step at a time.

When we got home from that appointment I went to the hospital with Kyle. We said good-bye to Uncle Paul. He passed away the next morning. The next few days were spent at his calling hours and his funeral. A historian for Montpelier, Vermont with many years in politics and theater, his service attracted hundreds of people. It was the most memorable funeral we had ever attended, complete with bagpipes and a parade. His daughter Kathryn had made all the plans – she honored him well.

In the midst of all that was going on Kyle gave her notice at work, packed, and was preparing for her move. She was so sad to loose Uncle Paul, and really upset that she wouldn't be home for Sherwood's surgery. She suggested not going, or postponing, but Sherwood wouldn't hear of it. She asked him if he would consider driving to Florida with her. He said he'd think about it. I know Kyle really wanted him to go. It would give her someone to share the driving, it would assure her of nicer hotels on the way, but most importantly it would give them time to talk. I doubted that in the end he would go – he just is not a traveler.

The next morning Sherwood surprised us all. He wanted to go on the "road trip" with Kyle. He would drive with her from Vermont to Orlando Florida. He'd fly home from there, and she'd continue the last leg of the trip alone. I was a little nervous. What if he flared up with another incident while they were on the road? The decision was his to make, and in the end it was the right one.

Kyle and Sherwood had a few very special days together on the road.

KYLE

I was once again saying good-bye to Mom. I could see real sadness in her eyes. I knew it was more than just me leaving this time. She was also worried about Dad – not just the trip, but the surgery that lay ahead of him.

We had spent the last few days loading my car, making hotel arrangements for the trip, and scheduling Dad's flight home. I know she was worried about that too. Dad wasn't a good traveler with someone else present, to say nothing about traveling alone. We had found a direct flight and I promised I'd see him off and wouldn't leave until I knew he was through security and sure of his gate. I knew Mom would call often during our trip. She did!

Dad and I had a great road trip together. We visited about Key West and his surgery, we laughed, we cried, and we reminisced. He talked about meeting me for the first time. I was only three years old sitting behind the counter of my mother's grocery store. He bought a newspaper and I rang it up. He had no idea then I'd be his daughter two years later. We've always been close - this trip brought us even closer.

I was so happy he had come along for the ride. I kissed him good-bye and watched him go through security and head to his gate. I called Mom to let her know he was on his way. She seemed to relax at least a little bit more with that news.

I arrived in Key West by early the next afternoon. I went to the manager's office and got the key to my Management Suite and my schedule. I'd be starting work in two days. Very exciting – a new start!

My first disappointment was the Management Suite. It was in a small hotel that the Westin had taken over. It had one small bedroom and bath with a living room area that served as a kitchen/dining area too. It was all very worn. It was next to the pool, so I considered this a plus. With a little TLC I would make this work.

I unpacked, made up my bed, and put a few personal things around. It was looking better already! The next two days were spent acquainting myself with the area, getting some groceries, and gearing up for my new job.

The area I was managing was on the island which meant I had to catch the 5:45 a.m. boat each day to get to work. That would mean getting up by 4:30 a.m.…this was going to be a different schedule than any I had been used to in the past.

It wasn't nearly as bad as I had expected. I settled in easily and the job was exactly what I expected. It was official, I was now a Floridian.

PATTY

I was happy Kyle had arrived safely in Key West and was now settled in. It was one less thing to worry about, although I worried if she would be happy.

Sherwood's surgery was scheduled. I checked him in and Sherri came to the hospital to wait with me. The surgery would take about four hours. My phone continued to ring with the other kids checking in on him. My friend Cathie showed up with Champlain Chocolates – if nothing else a little chocolate was sure to cheer me. It was a delicious distraction!

The surgery was over and we were summoned to a small office. The doctor told us that the surgery went as expected. Everything looked good. They had removed two small tumors which they would send away to get tested. Sherwood could leave in a few hours. What a relief! Our next appointment for follow-up and results was scheduled.

When the doctor said no surprises and everything looked good I felt as if we were in the clear. Our next appointment proved otherwise. Sherwood has bladder cancer. I am a note taker. I know that sounds weird, but it's what I do. It helps me focus. So, as the doctor is telling us the results I'm writing down everything he says. If I hadn't I probably wouldn't have heard anything other than "he has cancer." I was in shock. Sherwood was not. He had been expecting it. He knew that nearly 50 years of smoking would eventually catch up with him. More appointments were scheduled. We would soon be learning about our options.

I called each of the kids that night and told them what we had learned. It was very sad.

They had told us that Sherwood had a very aggressive form of cancer. We had choices, and we elected aggressive surgery. He would have his bladder, lymph nodes, and prostate removed. It was a very major surgery. He was scheduled to go into the hospital on his birthday May 12th.

Sherwood wanted to go to Key West and see Kyle. He always felt better when he could see in his head where she was living and working. Our trip had been scheduled for late April. We went. We stayed at a beautiful little Bed and Breakfast owned by the Westin. It was in the Truman Annex, an old Victorian house – our room was on the top floor with a balcony overlooking the Annex. It was lovely. We had a great few days with Kyle. While we were there we helped her give some life to her living quarters by buying plants, a beautiful piece of art, new bedding, and slip covers for the arm chairs. It actually was quite cute when we were done.

We were glad to have made the trip. Sherwood was feeling good and we had a great time. Although we knew when we returned home we had a major surgery to face.

KYLE

I was devastated when I heard Dad had cancer, and even more upset when I realized the extent of the surgery he would be having. He had always been so proud of how he looked, and how he dressed. Now in place of his bladder he would have a urostomy, a bag on the outside of his stomach. I hoped he would be able to cope with the change. More importantly, I hoped he would come through the surgery safely.

Mom had told me that the surgery would either take two hours or eight hours. If they opened Dad up and the cancer had spread outside of the area, they would close him back up and not remove anything – which would mean that there was no cure. If it took eight hours it would mean things had gone as planned. I was sad I couldn't be there.

When Dad woke in the recovery room the first question he asked Mom was, "How long was I in surgery?" She told him eight hours, he smiled and went to sleep.

Recovery was difficult. Dad was in the hospital for more than a week. He was having the pain of the surgery, learning how to deal with his urostomy and for the first time in 50 years – not smoking. But, he recovered. That was the good news!

Mom called daily with an update and had a list of people that she would send email news reports to. Her messages were interesting to read. They were detailed and she tried to be light hearted with them. I swear it was their attitude, that positive approach to any situation that helped them through it.

Chapter XVIII

PATTY

The months following Sherwood's surgery were difficult. He was adjusting to his new body and not smoking. I was taking care of him and managing my business. I was grateful that I had him to take care of. It could have been so much worse.

I was fortunate to have gotten a contract that required a lot of writing, which allowed me to work at home through the summer with no travel. Once again I was grateful for having lost my job and starting my own business.

I continued to work with The Vermont Children's Aid Society, although I often felt frustrated. I was a Board member but I felt like I was putting in the effort of a full-time employee. I was still chairing the Development Committee, and I was on the Executive Board. We were approaching their 90th anniversary so I was also involved with that committee. I was starting to feel overwhelmed by the load I was carrying!

We did have some great news that June. Keith and Julia had a little boy, Kellen. Our family was growing. What a cute little family they were!

Kyle was finally dating someone. It was the first time in nearly two years that she had any interest in a guy. Evidently she was quite smitten, he was tall dark and handsome. Definitely the look she goes for.

In November the kids were planning a 25th Wedding Anniversary Party for us. It was going to be at Keith and Julia's restaurant, The Common Man. Kyle would be coming home, and her boyfriend would be joining her. We were anxious to meet him!

KYLE

I was so excited to be going home for Mom and Dad's anniversary party. But I have to admit I was a little nervous bringing Chad home. My mother's family can be over powering. I was hoping they'd go easy on him, and that he would like them. The funny part was he really didn't know what was in store for him I had been a bit vague. I didn't want him to be nervous!

Mom was at the airport to greet us with open arms. She seemed to hit it off with Chad instantly, although she gets along easily with everyone. I was also anxious to see how Dad would react. He was a little more reserved, but everything seemed ok!

The anniversary party was amazing. It was small, mostly family with a few close friends. A fun country band played, it was nonstop dancing, laughing and fun. I had never seen my parents have so much fun! Dad looked great. He looked healthy and happy. It was good to be together again.

The trip was short, but sweet. Chad survived meeting the family, and I was so happy to have had time at home.

PATTY

Sherwood and I had the time of our lives at our anniversary party. The next day our bodies were tired from all the dancing. It will definitely go down in our history as one of our best days ever.

It was great to see Kyle and meet Chad. His personality wasn't exactly what I expected, he was nice enough, and he obviously adored Kyle, but there was something I wasn't sure I liked. But, if Kyle is happy, I'm happy.

Evidently everyone else didn't have quite the same sentiment. Chad didn't score big on the family front. Everyone attributed it to meeting so many people all at once and trying to fit in, which would be tough for anyone.

Over the course of the next few months their relationship grew and Kyle seemed more her old self again. It was a relief. You tend to worry less about your kids when they are with someone that you know loves them.

KYLE

My relationship with Chad is growing. He wants to move in together. I'd love to get out of this Management Housing and I would love to be with him, but am I ready for that level of commitment?

Our relationship had a very romantic start. If there were issues along the way it was usually with me. I found I had built a defensive barrier around myself and was having trouble letting Chad in. I know I was just protecting myself, but little things I would do, little defenses I would put up would hurt his feelings. I was going to try harder to change. I felt I wasn't being fair to him.

Together we found a great condo to rent. Work was going fine for me. Chad talked about starting a dive business. He had his captain's license and was a certified scuba instructor. He knew it would be successful. He just needed to make the investment and commitment to get it going. The fact he had no personal capital didn't seem to be a concern.

I asked Mom to help Chad put together a business plan. He presented the business plan to his parents. It took some convincing, but they helped him get the boat. By summer, to coincide with the sinking of the Vandenberg, he was in business. There were a lot of expenses that went into starting a dive business – dive equipment, marketing materials, a web-site, docking the boat – the list seemed endless. But it was Chad's dream, and I believed in him, so I supported us while he got established. Things seemed to be going quite well.

As one part of my life seemed to be finally on track, Mom called with some news that I was not prepared for. During a routine pet scan they found a spot on Dad's lung. He was going to now undergo another surgery – almost one year from the date of his last operation. I was distraught. We talked about me going home to be there and in the end decided I'd come following the surgery to be with him during his recuperation.

PATTY

I made a point of going to all of Sherwood's doctor's appointments with him. I wanted to hear what the doctors had to say, and I wanted to ask questions – since I knew that he probably would not. I was not prepared for our April appointment. Evidently they had seen a spot on his lung that appeared to be growing. They wanted to remove half of his left lung. We were devastated. As is my custom, I busily wrote down notes and listened to the details.

When I got home I called each of the kids. I hated sharing such difficult news with them. This was a major surgery and it was not going to be easy.

There was no place to go but forward. The surgery was scheduled, they removed half of his lung, and while they were inside him they discovered another spot on the upper lobe, they removed that, as well as the surrounding lymph nodes. The surgery went as well as could be expected. The recovery was slow.

I was so proud of how Sherwood handled everything that came his way. He never complained, he simply endured. Our next appointment with the doctor was a significant blow. They had found cancer in his lymph nodes. He was going to have to begin chemo immediately. The chemo would not make him better, but it was possible that it might prolong his life if it could stop the cancer from spreading. My mind went blank, but I kept writing notes, capturing all of the details. In August of 2009, we were told he probably had one year to live. Chemo would begin as soon as he was fully recovered from the surgery.

Kyle and Chad came home to visit. As sad as our news had been the worse was seeing Kyle and Sherwood hugging and her crying with him. I think it may have been harder on her than the other kids simply because she wasn't able to be there. But she was here now and he was doing really well. He felt good and he was looking good.

We heard all about the business, and were frankly a little surprised Chad had chosen to come to Vermont with Kyle since his new business was just taking off. He seemed very positive and enthusiastic about the business. Kyle on the other hand seemed a little down. I thought it was because of Sherwood, but soon learned that she was stressed with life in general. She thought she was in love with Chad but she wasn't happy with his nonchalant approach to the business. He came from a family of means and seemed to rely on them more than he should. She had also accumulated a small debt helping him get started. He had his dream, now it was time for him to make it work. She realized it would take time – she'd give him time.

KYLE

I loved being home with my family again. We spent most of our time at the cottage on the lake. I loved the calming effect of the lake, I always have. Just being there I felt better.

Dad looked good. Mom was her usual happy go lucky self. Although I knew she was concerned over Dad's health she always wore a brave face. They were both amazing.

Dad has never been good at hiding his feelings. It was apparent before the end of our trip that he was not one of Chad's biggest fans. That bothered me. I wasn't sure if it bothered me so much that he didn't like him, or that it made me begin questioning things about him myself, things that I had been privately thinking about.

Time would tell.

PATTY

It was great having Kyle home again, but I wish she had come alone. Having Chad with her was adding a tension that normally would not have been there. He was arrogant and controlling. Two traits I didn't like, and hadn't really noticed until now.

I spoke to Kyle about life. She was not as happy as she should be for someone newly in love. It seemed she was working awfully hard to make it work. She did not want another failed relationship.

Regardless, we enjoyed our time together. I can never get enough Kyle time. I hated to see her leave, although I had plenty to keeping me busy.

I was taking care of Sherwood, working hard at my business, and planning the 90th Anniversary Event for The Vermont Children's Aid Society. The 90th Event was the week before chemo began – so it was a good distraction. It went beautifully. We were able to raise another $12,000 through a silent auction and donations. I again shared Kyle's story to let them know not only how I got involved with Vermont Children's Aid Society but the difference her events had made to the organization. The Kids-A-Part Program, which she funded, had become nationally recognized and was now being used as a model for other states. Two beneficiaries of Vermont Children Aid Society services spoke. Their stories were very moving. The event was a success!

Sherwood's chemo began the next week. We were pleasantly surprised with the reaction Sherwood was having. He didn't get sick and he didn't lose his appetite. Everything seemed great. Until later that weekend when I found myself dialing 911. He had passed out in the bathroom. As it turns out he had a bleeding ulcer from all the medication he was on and probably from the stress he was under. It was scary. I was so afraid we had just gotten a glimpse of what our next year would be like.

Sherwood had two more chemo treatments before his next pet scan. When we went for the fourth treatment they decided not to give it to him. There was no need to continue the chemo, they said, because it was not working. The cancer had spread to his bones, and his stomach. My notes included all of the details, which was good since I didn't remember hearing anything past the words "the chemo isn't working."

I was so sad. Sherwood was so calm. He had been expecting this. I had not.

KYLE

I often wondered how she did it. When Mom called to tell me the latest news on Dad she was very calm and matter of fact. I could hear the pain in her voice, but she never wavered. She shared with me the conversations they had and assured me they'd be fighting it until the end. I didn't handle the news as well. I cried for days.

The next day Dad called to talk to me. The call was special. He wasn't one to initiate a phone call, but he wanted to assure me that for now he was living. He didn't want me sad and worrying about him. Although his phone call could never have changed my being sad and worried, it did help me feel better hearing the calmness in his voice, and the love.

I called often to speak to Mom and Dad. I wanted to make sure everyone really was ok. Mom and I planned a surprise for Dad. His favorite holiday is Thanksgiving, I was going to fly home and surprise him. Keith and Julia would have the whole family to their house for dinner – all of the children and grandchildren would be together. I decided to come home alone. Chad would stay and work the business.

I arrived two days before Thanksgiving. My flight came in late at night. Dad was in bed when I arrived. In the morning I heard him in the kitchen making coffee. I came up to ask him if he had another cup. He was in shock. The expression on his face was worth the trip. He hugged me and cried. He was so happy I'd come home to be with the family for Thanksgiving. He said it would be his best one ever…and I'm sure it was.

Once he got over the shock of my arrival the first question he asked is if I would go with him and help him shop for Mom's Christmas gifts. One of our traditions could take place again this year.

It was so good to see Dad and spend time talking with him. He looked great. He didn't look like a man who was dying. I did notice he was more tired than normal. Bed came early and he slept late. Other than that he seemed like his normal self.

The three of us went out to dinner, we had our family Thanksgiving at Keith's, and Dad and I had our shopping date. He bought Mom a beautiful diamond solitaire necklace, I knew she would love, and lots of clothes.

The night before I left I found a surprise on my pillow. Dad had gone back to the jewelry store, on his own, and bought me a beautiful amethyst and diamond necklace that had taken his eye earlier. He wanted me to have a lasting piece of jewelry from him. I'll cherish it always!

Mom and I had a few heart to hearts while I was home. She sensed I wasn't feeling positive about my relationship or a future with Chad. I was stressed from my job and trying to make ends meet, supporting both of us. Key West was loosing its appeal. I had been trying to be happy, and I was hoping Chad would be part of that happiness. But right now I just wasn't feeling it. On top of all that she was dealing with, I hated to add to Mom's stress with my issues, but she knows me so well there was no chance we weren't going to have these conversations.

PATTY

It was the perfect Thanksgiving. All of the kids and grandkids were together, Sherwood was beaming, and cameras were clicking! We were sure to take lots of pictures we wanted to capture the memory forever.

I loved being with Kyle but I hated seeing her unhappy. She felt as though leaving Chad would mean starting over yet again. She did love him, but it didn't feel right – it didn't feel like enough. These were tough decisions that only she could make. All I could do was let her know we loved her and would support whatever decisions she made.

I hated seeing her go, but we had a huge trip scheduled together in February. My nephew, Scott, was going to be married in Hawaii. We'd go together. Unclear of how Sherwood would be, I purchased travel insurance, just in case he wasn't feeling well by then.

As it turned out Sherwood was doing great and was thrilled that Kyle and I would be having a trip together. He knew that our passion was travel, and that we both needed the strength of each other right now.

KYLE

My mother called it "The Perfect Storm." I was feeling miserable – I realized that as much as I wanted to love Chad, he was never going to be the man I wanted him to be. Then I asked my boss if I could have 10 days off to go to Hawaii and was told that I couldn't because of a big project taking place at the resort that week. I went home a little depressed, only to get a call from my girlfriend from California asking whether I would consider coming back to San Diego to help her manage her new restaurant.

Over the course of the next few weeks I made decisions that definitely would impact the rest of my life -- my mother's words of guidance ringing in my head: be brave, be strong, be proud – I believe in you. I've heard those words so many times before!

I gave my notice at work. I asked Chad to leave. I accepted the job with Lisa, and I started planning my move back to California. I made plans to drive to Vermont where I'd spend some time with family before I left for the west coast.

I would leave the week after returning from Hawaii.

PATTY

Off to Hawaii. Sherwood was feeling good. I had just completed a big job for a major insurance company. I was traveling with sisters, and soon would be with Kyle. I was happy.

Kyle and I shared a room with my sister Kathy. The three of us had a great time. We kept it light and didn't spend a lot of time focused on the negative things in life. We were on vacation after all.

Still, as hard as you try, you can't just forget about everything else that is going on in life. I missed Sherwood. And even though I had kids alternating times with him while I was away, I still hated leaving him for 10 days. Kyle was sad that her relationship with Chad didn't work out, and it looked like she was going to have to carry debt she acquired so he could have his business – the prospects of him paying her back were bleak. We both had heavy weights we were carrying. Being together helped us both deal with whatever lied ahead.

KYLE

The trip to Hawaii was perfect. Mom and I both needed the release. I was thankful that she didn't push conversations about my relationship. We had a lot of time to talk. We spoke about Dad and the changes we all would be experiencing in time. My heart was in turmoil. I wanted the time to quickly pass so I could move on and get over this relationship, but I also wanted it to slow down so we could have more quality time with Dad.

The ten days went quickly. As great as Hawaii was, it was even greater driving out of Key West when I returned. I felt a huge pressure lifting from me when I got behind the wheel and headed north.

I was closing a chapter on another part of life. I wasn't sure what was ahead of me but I did know that I was making the right decision. I was happy to have ended my relationship with Chad before it had gone any further, before a wedding, before a child. When it is my time I will find Mr. Right and I will have all that I have dreamed of.

For now I am happy with me. I don't know where life will take me from here, but my heart is open!

Epilogue

PATTY & KYLE

Sherwood Charles Carbee died quietly and peacefully in his sleep on Friday morning, October 8, 2010. He was our husband, father, mentor, friend – and the quiet presence that gave us the strength and courage we needed to get through the ups and downs of the past few years. Always there to lend support, give a hug, offer advice, or just listen, Sherwood had always been, and remained until the day of his death, the one constant we could count on.

He lost his battle with cancer the same way he lived his life: with strength, dignity, and acceptance. Never one to complain, he was there for us to the end…more worried about our feelings and whether we were going to be okay than the pain and sickness he was suffering. We will always love him for that, and we will miss him terribly.

******

**Patty, Sherwood and Kyle enjoying our last dinner out as a family
– a loving memory.**

PATTY

The water is still, the sun is shining bright and in time, I know
I'll be okay. Tonight, I looked once again out over the expanse of
Lake Champlain, and for the thousandth time remembered my father's
words: Vermont is God's Country, the most beautiful place on earth.

I still don't know what this journey of life is all about, nor where it
will take me in the years to come. But regardless of all that has and all
that might yet happen, I will continue to keep a positive attitude. If I've
learned anything over these past few years, it's that life truly is what you
make of it. And I too will work toward the happy ending.

By my side through Sherwood's death and the months that followed
was Kyle, providing her love and support. Having her with me was a
blessing.

We have found that together we are strong!

Patty and Kyle – Authors

Patty Carbee and Kyle Paxman are mother and daughter. Their roots are in Vermont. This is their first book. Together Strong is a story of a canceled wedding and the events that followed, told from both the mother's and the daughter's perspective.

Pictures by photographer Andrew Sawtell.